Runaway He

Joanna Thompson

Runaway Hearts

Planet Girl

The Morning After the Day Before

There's a running joke in my family and it goes something like this: my East German father slept through the Berlin wall coming down. Yes, while thousands of people lined up to laugh and cry and smash the wall that had divided their country for so long, Dad just went to bed. All of his friends went down to the **border**, *all of them*. Aber Papa "war ganz schön müde". We often laugh at him about this. Dad missed making history to go to bed – ha!

Well, I'm never going to be able to laugh at him again, that's for sure. My name's Emily Hausmann and I'm my father's German-English daughter. Chalk Farm School for Girls, my very own Berlin wall, fell yesterday – Miss Bardwell left the school. Miss Bardwell was my Latin teacher, **housemistress** and **evil** dictator rolled into one. She **resigned**, effectively opening up our lives to freedom and sunlight. Girls here at our London boarding school stayed up totally late in the **common rooms** last night, partying quietly and dancing into a new **era**.

But me? I wasn't celebrating. I wasn't at any party. I just

+++ border – Grenze +++ housemistress – Hausvorsteherin +++ evil – böse +++ to resign – kündigen +++ common room – Gemeinschaftsraum +++ era – Zeitalter +++

wanted to get some *zzzzs*. I slept through it all. Which is a bit ironic as I was *sort of* the reason Miss Bardwell left. So when I wake up on The Morning After the Day Before, it actually takes me a minute to remember. It's over. *She's gone.*

Miss Bardwell didn't actually *hate* me, I don't think. She *had* always hated my aunt Nora. They were at school here together many moons ago, when Miss Bardwell was a **spotty**, ugly teenager (I've seen the photos, trust me) and my aunt was a beautiful, funny one. Miss Bardwell certainly didn't *like* me very much but the fact that my rich English grandmother – the late Queen Mother, **God rest her soul** – was a bit of cash machine for the school protected me.

When the Queen Mother went off to the giant tearoom in the sky a few months ago, it was like my **lucky charm** had gone. And when Miss B's **fiancé** Mr Michaels fell in love with Nora and **dumped** Miss Bardwell suddenly, it was like I was stuck in a giant game of Mortal Kombat: Miss Bardwell vs my Auntie Nora and me. Everything exploded at my grandma's **funeral** where Miss Bardwell told Nora that she had killed her mother. Charming.

After that, I just found I couldn't take it any more. I couldn't sit in class with a frozen smile while Miss Bardwell **carried on** acting like she was queen of the school, making bad jokes and laughing at any girl who dared to

+++ spotty – pickelig +++ God rest her soul – Gott hab sie selig +++ lucky charm – Glücksbringer +++ fiancé(e) – der/die Verlobte +++ to dump s.b. – mit jmdm. Schluss machen +++ funeral – Beerdigung +++ to carry on – weitermachen +++

be a bit poor or stupid. And I *really* couldn't **stand** it when Miss Bardwell decided, one bright day, to make her pet, Amanda "Cyclops" Dobson, a prefect. Amanda's our in-house Superzicke here in Kensington house. (She's a bit like Miss Bardwell's younger and prettier evil twin.)

When it was clear that Miss Bardwell planned to "elect" Amanda herself, I organised a little protest. I put forward my own *Gegenkandidatin,* nice guy Sadie Reece, my roommate. And when Miss Bardwell ignored our "democratic candidate", we striked.

It's true. Nearly all the boring, horse-crazy, rich girls in my class actually agreed to boycott Latin. Miss Bardwell **went nuts**: actually, she went nuts in front of "the press". "The press" were Nora, who's the best photographer in the world, **incidentally**, and who came to take pictures of all the pony-club revolutionaries. Oh, and Chris, who was there to report what happened. Perhaps I should also mention that he's like the best kisser in the world? The best thing in the world?

Note to self: I must not think that. Here's what Chris actually is: he's an **intern**, a trainee journalist at *The Sentinel*, the newspaper Nora works for. I met him when Nora got me a job "helping" out there in the photography department. I'm as crazy about taking photos as Nora is, though sadly only about 1/18th as talented.

There were two things I noticed about Chris straight away: when God was giving out hair, Chris was not kept

+++ to stand s.th. – etw. ertragen/aushalten +++ to go nuts – durchdrehen +++ incidentally – übrigens +++ intern – Volontär/in +++

waiting in line for long. Man, he's one hairy **dude**. "Jack Wolfskin" my friend Maudie calls him. I also spotted **at once** that Chris has principles where other people have white blood cells. He seemed so *serious* about *everything*.

Chris being so serious about everything made me think that he must be about 58. It was a shock to discover later that he's only 17, just two years older than me. It was around the same time I noticed that Chris was "Teenwolf" and not "Opawolf" that I realised two other things about him: when God was handing out beautiful eyes, Chris was also at the front of the queue. And he's kind. He was lovely to me when I cried one day at the paper about Grandma. I do like a kind boy.

I suppose it was after noticing all of those things that I really started to think that maybe the idea of us being together wasn't *completely* crazy. It is, of course, still a totally **bonkers** idea. Nuts. **Insane**. Almost as insane as me kissing him.

Yes, I kissed him. It happened after Miss Bardwell went **loco** at our little "demo", **slapping** Nora and screaming that she would burn down *The Sentinel* and so **detonating** her own career at Chalk Farm. Chris and me took Nora home to recover and after she went to bed, we found ourselves alone on her sofa. It must have been the shock …

The shock, yes, let's **blame** the shock! It was the shock,

+++ dude – Kerl +++ at once – sofort +++ bonkers – meschugge +++ insane – verrückt +++ loco – verrückt +++ to slap – *hier:* ohrfeigen +++ to detonate – zerstören +++ to blame s.th. – etw. die Schuld geben +++

naturally, that made me throw myself on top of Chris and start kissing him. He did *definitely* kiss me back, by the way, but he also pushed me off him as well. Not a good sign. And I just knew that he was going to tell me something I really didn't want to hear, so I ran from Nora's flat. *Run, Emily, Run.*

I haven't heard a thing from Chris since. At one level, that's not a total surprise as he doesn't actually have my phone number. At another level – he does have my e-mail address – it is a bit sad. OK, it's not just a bit sad, it's a flaming *tragedy*.

I have been trying really, really hard not to think about hairy, principled, **gorgeous** Chris. That wasn't exactly hard yesterday: my **schedule** was packed. After I'd arrived back at school, I **barely** had a second to think. We had one afternoon class where our headmistress Mrs Randall announced that Miss Bardwell had resigned and that Sadie was officially our new prefect. Hurrah! Then we were all set free early and my afternoon looked like this:

First on the agenda: "celebration" plate of chips in White Out, my favourite café, with our now world-famous new prefect. Sadie was always one of the quieter girls in our class, easy **prey** for someone like Cyclops. And now she's suddenly super-confident and hyper-active. She's like one of those toys you had kicking around your bedroom as a kid that never seemed to actually do anything until your mum finally remembered to put batter-

+++gorgeous – wunderschön +++ schedule – Terminplan +++ barely – kaum +++ prey – Beute +++

ies in it one day and PING! You suddenly couldn't stop it. Sadie and me are actually roommates in dorm 3B together so we could have had our "strategy talk" there. But Sadie insisted on buying "the best campaign manager in the world" (erm, me, surprisingly) dinner as a thank you. Normally I'm anyone's for a plate of chips but not yesterday. Every time I thought of Chris, I felt like I was going to **throw up**. Sadie ate most of my chips for me. She not only did all the eating, she did all the talking, too, chatting enthusiastically about all the changes she wanted to make. Like: "prefects having a listening hour, when pupils can tell us about anything that needs changing at the school! The first thing I'd change myself …"

But I didn't listen to anything else about the listening hour, ironically. I was listening to my heart, which was, of course, thinking about Chris again. I was just starting to remember how his lips felt on mine when I noticed Sadie was **nodding** at me, and looking like she was waiting for some kind of answer. "So you'll help me out with that?" she said. I suddenly had the feeling she was repeating herself.

She was smiling at me **eagerly**, pushing her glasses manically up and down her nose, and I mumbled quickly, "Oh absolutely! No problem!" even though I had no idea what I'd just agreed to. It's a bad **habit** of mine, I should perhaps mention. It usually means trouble.

+++ to throw up – sich übergeben +++ to nod – nicken +++ eagerly – eifrig +++ habit – Gewohnheit +++

Anyway, after agreeing to whatever-it-was-I-just-agreed-to, I rushed off to my 5 pm **appointment**. It was an emergency post-crisis meeting in Bloomsbury house with my best London friends Kim and Maudie. They were both "burning" to know what had just happened in Kensington. Kensington is Chalk Farm's most boring house and they're not normally "burning" to hear about anything going on there. But yesterday we Kensington girls could hold our heads up high. Our house was finally the place to be, a **hotbed** of revolution and excitement, rock 'n' roll central.

+++ appointment – Verabredung +++
hotbed – Brutstätte +++

We met in the Bloomsbury common room and as I walked in, Maudie and Kim **mobbed** me, like I'd just won *Pop Idol* or something. They wanted to know everything at once, every detail. *Where exactly did Miss Bardwell hit Nora? Like here on the* ***cheekbone*** *or more on the mouth?* And so on. Kim even **insisted on** getting me a cup of tea. I could get used to this! It was like being famous for a day.

So I gave them an exclusive interview: they hung on my every word. When I'd finally finished, Kim sighed, "I can't believe it." She was sitting in a huge **burgundy** armchair, looking a bit like one of those little ballerinas that you get inside music boxes, even tinier and prettier and blonder than usual. "Bardwell's actually gone! And Cyclops? What's she saying about it all?"

"There's nothing on her Facebook page about it," grinned Maudie. Maudie has been a bit **obsessed with** Cyclops, ever since she had a boy stolen by her. I actually had a bit of a fight with Maudie recently about, well, her obsessive behaviour. Not just the Cyclops cyber-watch thing: I had also tried to warn Maudie about being too possessive of her boyfriend Matt. But I made a mess of it and Maudie got angry with me. She finally forgave me by **text** a couple of days ago – after Matt himself told her the same thing I had. We hadn't really discussed it girl-to-girl yet, though.

+++ to mob s.b. – über jmdn. herfallen +++
cheekbone – Wangenknochen +++ to insist on s.th. – auf etw. bestehen
+++ burgundy – burgunderrot +++ to be obsessed with s.th. –
von etw. besessen sein +++ text – SMS +++

Maudie was clearly thinking about our stormy personal history, too. “But really,” she said quickly, rubbing her spiky **hedgehog** hair, “I’m over all that – watching Cyclops and … Matt all the time. You were right, Emily, I need to get my life back and stop worrying.”

She laughed. She looks amazing when she laughs, Maudie. She has the best smile, a really warm, wonderful one, that makes you instantly just want to laugh along with her, even if she were actually telling you that she had never liked you, ever.

“So, I’m sorry about everything,” she said **gently**. She leant across and gave me a **hug**, which was a bit tricky as we were sitting a metre apart on two separate chairs. “I should’ve listened to you … basically Matt said the exact same thing you did. I was *seriously uncool* for a while there.”

“You’re never uncool,” I said. I meant it. Just look at her **adorable** *Vokuhila* and seven piercings!

We all laughed again, **relieved.** Kim sipped her tea thoughtfully. “And what about Jack Wolfskin? What did he make of all these crazy girls? Is it going to be in the newspaper?”

“No,” I said slowly. “I think Chris was just going to write up what happened in his … blog.”

It hit me at the very split second that the word *blog* left my mouth. His *blog*. I hadn’t even checked it yet! I mean, it’s not like I *seriously* expected Chris to send me a mes-

+++ hedgehog – Igel +++ gently – sanft +++ hug – Umarmung +++ adorable – anbetungswürdig +++ relieved – erleichtert +++

sage via his blog. **Obviously** not. That would be too much to wish for. Still, it couldn't hurt to *check*.

I managed not to be *totally* **rude** to Maudie and Kim but I did rush off rather quickly after saying the word "blog". I told the girls that I was tired – and then made that totally unbelievable by racing at Usain-Bolt-like top speed all the way along the hall, down the stairs, back up the stairs and into the Kensington computer rooms.

I'd looked at Chris' blog before, of course. It's not really totally exciting. There are no pictures of him kite surfing in Peru or doing crazy stunts. It's all dry stuff about working at the newspaper and more information on any news stories he's interested in.

Yesterday, though, it was fascinating! Chris' account of the whole day was already online, as were a couple of Nora's photos of us all. The school and Miss Bardwell weren't actually named – there's simply a story about a teacher "hitting" a "well-known photographer" in an attack following a protest by pupils. And I couldn't help but notice that I also wasn't named.

Everyone else who was there yesterday got a mention it seems: Melissa and Sadie. Oh brother, even Becks, my other roommate, was in there! But me – the organiser of the strike, the brains behind the whole operation, *the girl he kissed* – not a thing. I've been disappeared.

Chris is a serious journalist, of course! He's not exactly

+++ obviously – offensichtlich +++
rude – unhöflich +++

going to write: "And then I went back to the well-known photographer's flat and kissed her **niece**." But somehow I had hoped that he'd at least say something like: "Emily Hausmann, the spiritual leader of the revolution, has inspired the girls at Chalk Farm with her natural charisma and leadership." No, not really.

Oh well, even if he had **censored** me, I should still **update** Chris. Professional **courtesy** and all that. I **hesitated** for about 0.8 seconds then I sent a quick mail to the address on the blog. *Dear Chris, Just thought you'd like to know that the "teacher" resigned today and has already left the school. Emily.*

That was fairly cool, wasn't it? I'd love to have added something like: *when will I see you again?* Or *I haven't stopped thinking about you.* But I didn't.

+++ niece – Nichte +++ to censor – zensieren +++
to update – auf den neuesten Stand bringen +++
courtesy – Höflichkeit +++ to hesitate – zögern +++

The Smell of Relationship

So, like I said, that was yesterday. I was so depressed after reading the blog that I avoided all the parties and just went to bed. It's now the day after *la revolución* and it's time to face the music. The kiss at Nora's place might have been the most exciting kiss of my life but there's no escaping the fact that *Chris pushed me off him*. I don't know why because I don't really know anything about Chris or his personal life. I know lots about his political value system. I know he loves the work of Helen Levitt, my favourite photographer. But other than that he might have been **raised** by wolves or *have a girlfriend already*.

I'm no relationship genius but I have a bit of a **sinking feeling** that might be why he pushed me away. Chris is 17 and he's **cute**: it would be surprising if he *didn't* have a girlfriend. I wonder how I can actually find out for sure. I once heard my roommate Melissa claim that she has a "nose" for **detecting** whether a guy has a girlfriend. She can "smell" on a boy whether he's already taken. She

+++ to raise – aufziehen +++ sinking feeling – komisches Gefühl +++ cute – süß +++ to detect – entdecken, herausfinden +++

thinks. And hey! Melissa had quite a long chat with Chris at the demo. He put her in his blog, remember! I wonder if she picked up on any "aroma".

I'm **desperate** OK, desperate! It's not going to be too hard to drop Chris' "smell" into the conversation with Melissa. Firstly because Melissa is now waking up in the bed next to me. She always gets up early to allow her to have some of the world's longest showers. (Not easy when you share a room with three other girls.) I only wake up early when I'm worried about something. Like *now*.

Melissa has sat up and is stretching out her arms. I can see she's wearing her favourite nightshirt – one that has an *actual real photo* of her hugging her horse Almonds. Melissa and Almonds are very close. Frighteningly close.

Luckily, once she's stopped stretching, all Melissa wants to talk about is the strike. It's mainly just a **string** of rhetorical questions: *Can I believe that Miss Bardwell has resigned? Can I believe that Sadie is a prefect?* She's soon on the subject of Nora and Chris. "What *did* happen after you and *whatsisname*, the journalist, took Nora back home, actually?"

I **blush**. No way am I telling Melissa that I kissed Chris! I manage to **mutter** a few things: "*Oh, we sat and held her hand, then Nora went to sleep* … And then I came back here to see what had happened and Chris went, erm, to the paper I suppose." It all sounds totally weak, even to my own ears, but Melissa just nods.

+++ desperate – verzweifelt +++
string – Kette +++ to blush – rot werden +++
to mutter – murmeln +++

Then she gets to her feet and says the magic and strangely awful words: "You can just *smell* girlfriend on him, of course. All the best guys *always* have **steady** girlfriends."

And, having destroyed any chance of my personal happiness, Melissa **skips off** into the shower, happily **humming** to herself: *Is it a sweet dream or a beautiful nightmare?*

It's just a *horrible* nightmare. There's nothing beautiful about this! I can't move from my bed. It's all too much to **bear**. I lie there and listen to the sound of running water and think about what Melissa said. I try to be a bit rational. Melissa's not a **mind-reader**, of course. She's not some kind of Love Sniffer Dog. It's not, actually, truly possible to be able to *sense* whether someone has a partner or not.

And yet, in my heart of sinking hearts, I know what Melissa means and I think she's probably right. Chris is certainly no playboy. So really that can only mean two things – either he's **way** too into his studies to have the time or energy for a girlfriend or he has one he met at a Greenpeace **rally** and is totally true to. Either way, I've got no chance. *None.*

I'm still lying in bed, busy with my love angst, when Melissa comes out of the shower again. She has a towel wrapped round herself and she's **shivering**. Chalk Farm might be a school for rich girls but they don't seem able

+++ steady – fest +++ to skip off – abhauen +++
to hum – summen +++ to bear – ertragen +++
mind-reader – Gedankenleser/in +++
way – *hier:* viel +++ rally – Treffen +++ to shiver – zittern +++

to afford heating here and it's freezing all year round – even in summer, bizarrely.

Melissa stares at me in surprise. I must look totally miserable. I just know she's about to ask what's wrong and, actually, I'm a bit afraid that if anyone is nice to me right now I'll start crying.

I need an emergency *Themenwechsel* – I really don't want anyone to know about Chris. Sadie and Becks are still asleep but the **rising bell** will sound in a minute. Panic! Then it hits me. There *was* an extremely weird moment yesterday that I had wanted to ask Melissa about. An extremely weird moment when it seemed like

+++ rising bell – Weckruf +++

I was seeing a *ghost*. The ghost of our ex-roommate, Olga Petrova.

"Melissa," I say quickly, "where's Olga right now?"

Olga was shipped home to America last year by her **billionaire** control-freak father and is supposed to be getting married soon. Not to the person she would like to be with – Josh, Melissa's brother – but to some rich boy named Taki. I had a very funny feeling that I saw Olga standing outside the school gates the day before yesterday, staring at us all as we had our photo taken by my Auntie Nora.

It's Melissa's turn to give me a **guilty** look. I know that she's **kept in touch** with Olga, even though they had a fight about Olga's relationship with Josh. I'm sure that Melissa knows where Olga is right now.

"Oh, erm, Florida, I suppose," says Melissa **airily**. "You know, she must be getting ready for her big day. Oops, forgot to put my deodorant on." And she disappears quickly back into the bathroom, leaving me wondering why Melissa – who never lies – would be lying to me now.

Hmmm. I can't be too **offended**, of course, because if Melissa's keeping secrets about Olga from me, I'm also keeping secrets about Chris from her. Fair's fair. Anyway, I'm still sure that it *was* Olga. The person I saw was wearing sunglasses and a hat, I have to admit, but there was something about her stare – diamond hard – that was

+++ billionaire – Milliardär +++ guilty – schuldbewusst +++ to keep in touch – in Kontakt bleiben +++ airily – vage +++ offended – beleidigt +++

100% Petrova. Well, even if she is back in town, she's not my problem. I was never really close to Olga. Ho hum.

The rising bell sounds and it's rush hour in the dorm as Sadie and Becks wake up. I get dressed and head off downstairs into the Brave New World that is Chalk Farm School without Miss Bardwell.

We should have Latin in the afternoon but it's, of course, cancelled, tragically. I think all the teachers in the school are trying to **adjust to** their new reality, too. No one actually seems to know what to do with us and we're told by Miss Shaw that we can have a free afternoon. Miss Shaw is our brilliant art teacher and she's going to take over as Kensington's new housemistress, hurrah! That should mean a lot more free afternoons, heh heh.

Freedom's **confusing** when you're not used to it, though. Two hours off in the middle of the day – I don't think I've ever had that here. I check my e-mails, of course, hoping that Chris might have replied. He hasn't.

Oh well. I'll see him at the weekend, maybe, when I normally go into *The Sentinel.* Although he's not always there at the weekend. *Oh man, I don't think I can stand this!* Having to wait till Saturday to see Chris, *when I might not even see him anyway.* It's suddenly **overwhelming:** *I could go to The Sentinel now.* I've got nothing to lose.

I change quickly out of my uniform and run straight to the underground. It's like I have a micro chip in my brain and I'm being **remote controlled** by someone who

+++ to adjust to s.th./s.b. – sich an etw./jmdn. gewöhnen +++ confusing – verwirrend +++ overwhelming – überwältigend +++ remote controlled – ferngesteuert +++

really wants me to see Chris. It's all I can think about. I'm suddenly full of hope: maybe I can apologise. Maybe we can start again. Maybe we're actually wrong about the girlfriend?

I'm in the lobby of *The Sentinel* in record time. I show my **ID badge** to Harry, the big-shouldered security man there, who grins at me. "You're not normally in during the week," he **chuckles**. "If you're looking for your aunt, she's not here today." I think briefly about asking Harry whether Chris is here, then decide it's too embarrassing. "I need to get something from Todd," I say quickly. Todd is the **art director**. I need a **cover story**, of course, and getting something from him will do.

I wonder guiltily where Nora is as I take the lift up to the 5th floor – I did try to phone her after the attack but I've only been getting her mailbox. I must ring her again soon. I hope she's **recovered** from being beaten up by the Bardwell. Ooh, she doesn't even know about Miss Bardwell leaving yet …

I've just realised that I'm not totally sure where I'm going. I've taken the lift automatically to the art and photography department but I don't really want to go there because Todd might actually get me to do a job for him. And I don't want to go to the newsroom where Chris would be if he's here. It would be too obvious.

I hesitate and then press the button for the top floor:

+++ ID badge – Mitarbeiterausweis +++
to chuckle – in sich hineinlachen +++
art director – künstlerische/r Leiter/in +++
cover story – Thema, Geschichte +++ to recover – sich erholen +++

the other place where Chris is regularly to be found is the cafeteria. I can go there and wait a while. I'll just take a seat somewhere central and **pretend** that I'm taking a break from researching something. If Chris does come in, he surely won't be able to ignore me. While I wait, I can calm my nerves and my aching heart with one of those **wicked** vanilla and blueberry muffins that they have here. It's a win-win situation.

I'm terrified when I walk into the cafeteria but, phew, I can see at once that Chris isn't there. So I do everything just as I planned. Operation Blueberry Muffin and Cappuccino. I take a brightly lit seat near the window where I'm pretty sure anyone walking in will see me. I get my mobile out and pretend to write important text messages. It's silly, of course. I don't even know that Chris is in the building and, even if he is, he might not come here.

But he does.

Chris walks in with a woman, unfortunately. A much older one, whose name I don't know but who I *think* works in the politics section. They're lost in conversation – about **domestic** education policy in the Sudan, no doubt – and Chris doesn't spot me right away. For a moment, I get to quietly admire him. He's wearing jeans. Plus a black **zip-up** fleece jacket. He's no clothes horse. But the black of his jacket sets off his eyes and he has this **pale** skin – did I mention his skin?

+++ to pretend – so tun als ob +++ wicked – super, genial +++ domestic – häuslich, inländisch +++ zip-up – Reißverschluss- +++ pale – bleich +++

I carry on admiring him. That's the easy part. I try to carry on drinking my cappuccino **casually**, too – that's the difficult part. I soon realise that I've got a drinking problem: I'm shaking too much to hold my cup. Chris and the woman are now collecting their trays. Oh, he's *never* going to see me. He hasn't even looked up! Once Chris gets started on a subject you can't stop him … Oh!

Just at that moment, Chris does **glance** up. He definitely sees me, *definitely*. His face turns even paler. Then he does a strange thing. He **frowns** and stares **beyond** behind my head at the window, rather as though he's seen a dead bird splattered on it. Then he looks down again at his tray and carries on talking to Politics Woman. They take a table at the other side of the cafeteria. I repeat – the other side of the massive cafeteria, **approximately** 800 km from my table. So it's like I'm in Siberia and they're in Holland or something.

That's it then. Brilliant. Chris totally blanked me. I feel absolutely **humiliated**. I slowly get up and leave the cafeteria.

I should be used to it by now, rejection, you'd think. It's my middle name. I've been treated this way before, by Ed Stanton, the first boy in London I liked and who dumped me by text. I thought I'd learned from that experience. I thought I'd grown and become a much better judge of character. The girl who fell in love with Ed was naïve. The

+++ casually – beiläufig +++ to glance – schauen +++
to frown – die Stirn runzeln +++
beyond – hinter +++ über etw./jmdn. hinaus +++
approximately – ungefähr +++ humiliated – gedemütigt +++

girl who fell for Chris was also naïve, it seems. Great progress, eh?

I **slump** back to school, I don't know where else to go. I do think for a moment about going to Nora's to see if she's there but I can't **face** telling her right now about Chris and I really can't bear the idea of sitting on the same sofa where I once had the best – and probably the last – kiss of my life.

I feel a **lump** in my throat. All I want to do is to go to the dorm and **crash out**. I'll stick my iPod on and ignore everything. Then my heart sinks: Betti, my friend back in Berlin, wanted to e-mail me tonight about a present I was to get Merle, another friend. It's some belt from a shop in Camden that Merle saw when they visited me here in London last Easter. Merle didn't have enough money to buy it then but still talks about it *all the time*. Betti's going to e-mail me the description of it. Merle's birthday is in a week so I'll have to go and find the thing tomorrow. She saw the belt six months ago now, of course, and looking for it is going to be a real waste of time, I know it. Why is *everything* complicated?

When I get into my account, the belt e-mail from Betti isn't there. An e-mail from Chris is.

Dear Emily, It was totally rude of me to ignore you today in the cafeteria and I'm really sorry. I just wanted to say that I'm totally sorry, too, about what happened at Nora's the other day. I do like and admire you very much. But I actu-

+++ to slump – *hier:* schleichen +++ to face s.th. – sich etw. stellen +++ lump – Kloß +++ to crash out – sich gehen lassen +++

ally already have a girlfriend so please can we keep it to ourselves? I hope we can still continue to work together and – as stupid as it sounds – still be friends. Congratulations on the strike again by the way. You're a true revolutionary. And I bet you're glad Miss Bardwell's gone. Chris

I don't write back. I start to but everything I try sounds **dumb** or, worse, heartbroken. What should I say anyway? And *keep it to yourself*? How hard is *that* going to be??? When your heart's been broken, it's your first instinct as a girl to rush off and tell your best friends. It's like a contract you sign when you're born female. It's cruel. It's like Chris is saying: *Kill all your beautiful memories, Emily. Line them all up and kill them one by one.*

+++ dumb – doof +++

The Sound of Silence

I'm just going to have to pretend that keeping your mouth shut is the new black. And weirdly enough, I'm going to get a brilliant chance to practice **being *en vogue*.** Sadie's first plan of action as a prefect is a sponsored silence of all things, to **raise money** for human rights activists in Russia!

I **groan**. I hate sponsored *anything*. I've **failed** at just about everything I've ever been sponsored for. A sponsored swim back in Berlin – I got cramp **in my second length.** I even had to stop doing a sponsored walk, getting the **blister** from hell within 20 seconds of starting. I'm useless. Now Sadie is really suggesting that we – a group of *großschnäuzige* teenage girls – all keep our mouths shut for *one whole day*.

To top it all, Sadie's claiming that I'd said I'd help *organise* the sponsored silence. In White Out, when I didn't eat my chips with her. I don't remember anything much about that day at all, except how sad I felt about well, life. The universe. OK, about Chris!

+++ to be en vogue – in sein +++ to raise money – Geld sammeln +++ to groan – stöhnen +++ to fail – versagen +++ in my second length – auf der zweiten Bahn +++ blister – Blase +++

So suddenly I have to do two things I *really* don't feel like doing: organising and being nice to people. "You have to convince people that it's a brilliant thing to do!" Sadie tells me, enthusiastically. "Our sponsored silence is symbolic of the **lack of** freedom of speech in Russia, of course." I nod flatly and Sadie yells, "Oh, come on! This is what we striked for, isn't it? To have prefects that actually do good things and don't just use their power to **boss** people **around**."

Was that why we striked? I think **dimly**. It all seems such a long time ago. It's like there was Life Before I Kissed Chris and Life After I Kissed Chris. But I have to help Sadie, of course. She's counting on me. "People listen to you," she tells me sincerely. "Sometimes. You're sort of cool."

So that's how I find my sort-of-cool-self standing next to Sadie in front of the class the following day. Sadie, who's suddenly become a Hillary Clinton *Powerfrau* overnight, tells everyone about human rights abuses in Russia and **Chechnya**. I just smile uncertainly and nod a lot.

It's **impressive**: Sadie certainly knows her stuff. Chechnya – now there's a place you *really* don't want to live/go on holiday to. All the girls are really quiet even, I notice, Cyclops. Can there actually be a heart under all that designer **underwear** of hers?

+++ lack of – Mangel an +++ to boss s.b. around – jmdn. herumkommandieren +++ dim – düster +++ Chechnya – Tschetschenien +++ impressive – beeindruckend +++ underwear – Unterwäsche +++

I watch Cyclops carefully as Sadie talks. We've been avoiding each other, Cyclops and me, since the showdown in the schoolyard. She actually looks, interestingly, rubbish, which is really unusual. Her hair has lost its incredible super glossy shine and her skin is **blotchy**. Weirdly, even her **dodgy** eye – the one that collided with a hockey ball – seems to have got bigger. It's like all her evil energy was sucked out of her when Miss Bardwell flew off on her **broomstick.**

And – even more amazingly – when Sadie and me hand out forms for the sponsored silence, Amanda takes one. She doesn't roll her eyes or say something bitchy about Sadie's glasses. Like I said – it's a crazy universe we're now living in.

"Please," trills Sadie as we walk round the room, "get your parents, friends, *whoever* to dig very deep in their pockets. We want to raise LOTS of money!"

Hmm. I consider whom I can ask to sponsor me. The Queen Mother is actually my first thought. Which is just *a bit* stupid, of course. Ah, Grandma. I still feel sad when I think about her. I have been wondering recently what she would have made of the strike and Miss Bardwell's resignation. And whilst I'm not glad she's dead or anything, I am *sort of* relieved that I don't have to tell her what happened. She would have *killed* me.

Then I suddenly realise that the Queen Mother also left what's called a "significant sum" to my parents in her **will.**

+++ blotchy – fleckig +++ dodgy – unstet +++
broomstick – Besenstiel +++ will – Testament +++

So they should definitely be good for a few euros! I have to call them anyway.

So EH phones home that evening. I ring Mum and Papa in their new massive villa, where they're sitting by the side of the pool, **sipping** their **daiquiris**. No, not really. I call them in exactly the same **humble**, rented flat in Prenzlauer Berg we've always lived in, though they are actually sitting on the new sofa that they finally got to replace the dirty **wobbly** one we had before. The sofa seems to be the only thing that they've actually bought so far with their **inheritance**. Or rather – my mother's inheritance. The Queen Mother didn't like my father and she didn't leave him so much as a bag of nuts.

My mother is obviously excited to hear my voice – well, no, I don't call her *every* week – and instantly agrees to sponsor me. 50 pounds! *Woohooh!* "It's a great cause," she says. "Nora will certainly give you something – did she tell you that she's going on **assignment** to Chechnya soon?"

Oh lord! After hearing all that stuff Sadie just told us about life there! I feel quite sick. Nora's *always* going to dangerous places to work. Why can't she ever take photos of *Markthallen* in Düsseldorf or somewhere?

Mum tells me that my little brother Max isn't at home, he's playing football. "But, oh, he really misses you!" she lies. Then my father comes on the line. He also seems really

+++ to sip – nippen an +++
daiquiri – alkoholischer Cocktail +++
humble – bescheiden +++ wobbly – wackelig +++
inheritance – Erbe +++ assignment – Auftrag +++

proud of my new social conscience and starts repeating a lot of the things that Sadie already told us about life in Chechnya. And then he laughs. "Aber sei mal ehrlich: die Klappe halten für 24 Stunden? Schaffst du niemals!"

Ooh. I'll show him! I hang up on my parents and instantly call Nora. I have to hear her voice. Maybe she's not really going to Chechnya. Maybe it's the Czech Republic?

Nora does actually answer her phone, amazingly. She's on the road, she says, can she call me later? She's heading to Nottingham, she tells me. "There have been some **riots** on a **housing estate** there, did you hear? Chris is covering the story, too. He says hi. He told me about Miss Bardwell – I want to hear *everything*. We'll talk soon." The line goes dead.

Oh nightmare! Riots, wow. Nora certainly does have an attraction to danger. And Chris is with her! Does that mean they'll be talking about me?

I hope they're both going to be OK. Riots. People throw things. Set fire to things. I realise that I'd actually rather be hurt myself than see anything happen to either Chris or Nora. Someone once told me that was the real definition of love. And yes, that's right, Emily Hausmann, the world's greatest **coward**, the girl who feels "pain" playing hockey in the rain, would actually take a **bullet** for *someone else.*

+++ riot – Unruhe +++
housing estate – Wohnsiedlung +++
coward – Feigling +++ bullet – Kugel +++

The day of the sponsored silence is here. Shhhh! I wasn't really excited about the idea of shutting up for so long at first. But actually, as a naturally lazy person, I am now quite glad that it's a sponsored event where I don't actually have to *do* anything. I've been promised nearly 200 pounds from my sponsors, too. As well as my parents, Maudie and Kim offered a share of their pocket money and I even got some of my old homies in Berlin to give me *ein paar Euro,* after I did a shout out on *SchülerVZ.* (Betti was so pleased that I actually remembered to get Merle's belt that she gave me 20 euros!)

The rules of the sponsored silence are that we're not to leave the school, unless it's an "emergency". The teachers have planned a "normal" school day – only with silent classes! It's totally cool. We have English with Mr Benn to start us off. He says, "Good morning, girls," in a cheery voice and we all wave back at him. **Hilarious**! Then he gives us a "Literature Quiz" to do. It's all quite relaxing for everyone, actually. Mr Benn looks happy sitting at his desk: he gets a newspaper out, *The Sentinel*! Ooooh! There's a picture on the front page that is *definitely* one of Nora's! I'd love to see if there's any mention of Chris.

So after the bell has rung, I go over to Mr Benn's desk. I can't actually ask him out loud if I can see *The Sentinel,* naturally, so I try using some hand gestures to indicate what I want. It doesn't work. Mr Benn just stares at me blankly until he finally gets impatient and says, "Oh, just write it down, Emily!"

+++ hilarious – lustig +++

I get out the little Hello Kitty notebook with pen attached that Maudie gave me for today and I write: *Could I see your paper, Sir? I think one of my aunt's photos might be on front page.* I don't write: *And I'm hoping there might be a story by the boy I* ***fancy***, of course. Mr Benn grins and passes the paper to me. I look carefully at the front page. There is indeed a picture of a burnt out house which says: *Photo: Nora Millington* underneath it. And next to it, under the headline: "SOCIAL ISOLATION **SPARKED** RIOTS" I notice that it says: *by Chris Morris.* Respect! I'll read it later online, I decide. Mr Benn plainly

+++ to fancy s.b. – auf jmdn. stehen +++
to spark – auslösen +++

wants his paper back: "I haven't finished the crossword." He's loving the sponsored silence!

Next, it's on to art where we have to be silently instead of noisily creative as we usually are. We're working with watercolours so I paint away **furiously**, trying to relax and not think about Nottingham. I do end up painting a car on fire, though. Still I'm starting to feel quite **zen**, actually. It's quite nice not having to make interesting conversation or clever jokes all the time. Who would have thought it.

Lunch time and a special **treat**: though we're normally not allowed to get our mobile phones out during the school day, Miss Shaw has given us special permission to use them so that we can text with each other a bit. I'm feeling positively **jolly** as I go to my dorm to get my phone. I'm even humming *The Sound of Silence* in my head as I switch it on and see that I have two messages. One is from Kim: *How's it going? Have you managed to keep your big German mouth shut?* Charming.

The other is from a number that my phone doesn't recognise. My heart falls backwards a bit. Chris? No. The message says: *Can you meet me this afternoon? Outside Archway Tube Station 5.30 pm? Urgent. Tell No One. Olga.*

I'm surprised and I'm not at the same time, of course. I was *sure* I'd seen Olga that day. Why does Olga want to see *me*, though? I suppose we did **bond** a bit during those terrible times together playing hockey in sub-zero tem-

+++ furious – wild, grimmig +++ zen – buddhistisch +++
treat – Vergnügen, Genuss +++ jolly – ausgelassen +++
to bond – *hier:* zusammenschließen +++

peratures. But generally I had the feeling that Olga never really warmed to me. I certainly never trusted her.

I'm desperate to know what's going on in her crazy life – *why is she here and not in Florida? Why is it urgent?* On the other hand, there will be large **amounts** of madness involved and I'm not sure if I want to get mixed up in that. And today of all days! I'm not allowed to talk. Even if I could get permission to leave school for a bit, I couldn't actually say anything to Olga. **There's no point in** going. None.

+++ amount – Menge, Anzahl +++
There's no point in ... – Es bringt nichts ... +++

Back from the Dead

Because I'm stupid and very **nosey**, I do go to meet Olga later, of course. I manage to convince Miss Shaw – in a Kitty note – that I have "urgent business" to attend to in town. I tell her some story about *my Auntie Nora having left her mobile somewhere and me needing to pick it up for her because she's in Nottingham.* It's a story that makes no sense when I think about it later but Miss Shaw just nods. "But, remember," she says, **winking**. "No talking! Otherwise, you'll have let everyone down. And straight back here!"

So off I silently skip. I'll just go and give Olga a note, explaining that I can't talk and that even if I could, I couldn't help her anyway. Simple. Strange but simple.

Archway is actually on the same line as Chalk Farm and it's a very weird trip I take there now. Normally in London *no one* ever talks to you. Your head could be on fire and nobody would even **bother** to warn you. But today *everyone* I pass wants directions or to know what the time is. I just shrug my shoulders and look **enigmatic**. It's quite entertaining.

+++ nosey – neugierig +++ to wink – zwinkern +++ to bother – sich die Mühe machen +++ enigmatic – rätselhaft +++

When I arrive at Archway underground station, I go up to the street level but can't see Olga straight away, which is unusual. She's a **stunning** blonde and you can normally spot her from a helicopter. She stops traffic, does Olga. Even in that stupid hat and glasses she had on the other day, I could still tell it was her.

And then I do spot Olga, standing on the opposite side of the street – I've come out at the wrong exit. She looks totally different to the way she did the other day. She's not wearing her sunglasses and hat "**disguise**" now and I can see that she's **dyed** her lovely blonde hair a funny sort of chestnut brown. She's still beautiful, of course. She's wearing a navy blue boyfriend blazer and some skinny jeans – classic Olga. Quietly expensive.

She's now standing, frozen to the spot near a lamp post. She doesn't wave back when I wave at her. She just looks around a bit jumpily and then stares straight ahead again. I cross the street. I've actually already prepared my note for her explaining about the sponsored silence but when I try to give it to her she just **hisses**, "Walk behind me. And don't talk." Well, that will be easy.

So we walk. We must look totally strange as I'm about half a metre behind Olga. We're together but not together. I have no idea where we're going. I hope it's not anywhere far. The weather is mild but it's going to rain, I can just *feel* it. I know those grey London clouds.

But we seem to march for days, or at least a good 15

+++ stunning – umwerfend +++ disguise – Verkleidung +++
to dye – färben +++ to hiss – zischen +++

minutes. Up a hill, no less … oh I've just realised where we are. Olga's taking me to Highgate **Cemetery**! Oh man, she's so weird and dramatic! A cemetery! What am I supposed to think now – *oh Olga's back from the dead or something*? And it's not just any old cemetery, it's London's most famous one. Karl Marx is buried here, for example. I want to shout out to Olga: *Can't we just meet in a nice warm café somewhere?* But of course I can't speak. I'm as silent as the grave, ho ho.

As we reach the gates of the cemetery, I'm powerless to stop us going inside. I read one of the signs quickly: Karl Marx is in the eastern section of the cemetery and Olga, I quickly realise, is taking us in that direction. She's walking confidently, rather as though she lived here. Maybe she's rented a **tomb** here to hide in.

Finally, after leading me past lots of graves and trees and bushes and after she's turned back on herself a few times, Olga stops next to a large tombstone shaped like an angel and turns to stare at me in that weird, spooky, Sphinx-like way that she has. Ah, how I've missed her.

I've had dreams that were less dream-like than this.

"Aren't you *ever* going to open your mouth, Hausmann?" says Olga suddenly. Her accent was always American but it sounds even more so now. She's really **drawling**: "I mean, I actually prefer you with your mouth shut but …"

I show her the note I'd already written: *Today is sponsored silence at school, can't talk.* Olga rolls her eyes. "Oh,

+++ cemetery – Friedhof +++ tomb – Grabmal, Gruft +++
to drawl – gedehnt sprechen +++

don't be so ridiculous! Who do you think is going to tell them you said anything? Karl Marx? The undead?"

Hmm. She *sort of* has a point, of course. But I did give everyone my word. I write down again: *We're raising money to help* ***oppressed*** *Russians!!*

Olga reads it and sighs. "Then I'm sure the school won't mind if you take a short break to help a Russian in **genuine** trouble. Honestly, Emily, I'm in real danger and you're being so selfish ..."

"OK, OK," I grunt. My voice feels strange, like it's a bit rusty now I haven't used it for, ooh, six hours. "So, well, what's going on?" I mumble.

Olga looks at me seriously. "What's going on? What's *going on* is I've run away from Florida because I don't want to marry someone I don't love. I want to stay here in London. I'm not going back to America. And I need your help!"

"Me?" I shriek. Why me? I'm not Olga's friend. I haven't spoken to her in a year! Why isn't Melissa standing here in a cold cemetery or ... Josh?? Josh would cut off his own hands to help Olga. He never got over her. Every second girl at Chalk Farm school seems to **have a crush on** him, but he's refused to date anyone else since Olga left.

Olga is staring at the sky, frowning. "It really is going to **bucket down** in a minute. Shall we go and find Uncle Marx? And on the way, I can tell you all about sunny Florida."

+++ oppressed – unterdrückt +++ genuine – wirklich +++
to have a crush on s.b. – in jmdn. verliebt sein +++ to bucket down – wie aus Kübeln regnen +++

Sunny Florida

When I'm feeling a bit guilty about it later – breaking my promise to my sponsors, I mean – I realise that I **hardly** said a word to Olga, not really. It was Olga who did 98% of the talking. And what a story it is.

Olga tells me everything: all about what happened after she left Chalk Farm, when her "Uncle Dimitri" arrived at Christmas to take her back to America. Taki, her fiancé, was waiting for her at the airport in Saint Petersburg (the one in Florida) with two dozen red roses. "And all I could do was cry when I saw him," she says flatly. "It was awful. I mean, Taki's *sort of* OK but I certainly don't want to marry him. I don't want to marry anyone! Who wants to get married when they're 16?"

I don't say Jamie Lynn Spears. I don't say anything. I'm too scared of Olga. But I mean, it is *sort of* funny. Of course Olga shouldn't be forced into marrying someone she doesn't love – that's awful. But it's not like Taki is Jabba the Hut or anything. Taki is a really **handsome** millionaire-to-be so I suppose, actually, there are probably *billions* of girls who'd like to be "forced" to marry him.

+++ hardly – kaum +++ handsome – gut aussehend +++

Luckily, I can't tell Olga that. "My dad is **nuts**," she continues. Then I do actually laugh nervously and she looks at me darkly. "You think I'm joking? He's been in and out of a psychiatric hospital for the past five years. He's **bi-polar**. He's terrifying. And one day I realised, if I didn't get away from him, my life would be over. It was quite spontaneous. I was at the mall looking at **table mats** with my mom and I left her in the shop while I went to the airport. I just ran."

I stare at my feet. My feet are cold is all I can think. I still can't see where this is going. How can I possibly help Olga? She needs … family. She must have some non-crazy people in her family.

"What about your mum? Didn't she understand?" I say quickly. Olga's stopped to stare at a particularly beautiful tombstone but she now looks back at me. It's a look I've seen before. It's a look that asks how it's possible that any human being can be quite as stupid as I am. "My mum doesn't care," she says shortly. "She just does what Dad tells her to. As long as he's sane enough to keep paying his credit card bills, she doesn't mind what he does. Plus, she loves weddings. She was totally into getting dresses and table decorations."

We've reached Karl Marx's grave. He's a friendly looking old guy, Mr Marx. Olga and me both stare at him. WORKERS OF ALL LANDS **UNITE** it says in gold on his tombstone.

+++ to be nuts – verrückt sein +++ bi-polar – manisch-depressiv +++ table mat – Untersetzer +++ to unite – sich vereinen +++

"That's the last line of The Communist Manifesto," says Olga absently. "I heard you'd become a bit of a revolutionary yourself, Hausmann, striking and things. I saw you all the other day."

"I knew it was you!" I say triumphantly. "Ooh, did you hear about Miss Bardwell?"

But Olga doesn't care about Miss Bardwell. She only cares about herself. She even says that: "Emily, this is about me. I want to just live the life I want to live. I'm 16 now, I'm an adult. That's really all I want. Except Josh."

Finally – Josh! I nod eagerly. Can't he stand here instead of me? But Olga kills that hope stone dead. She always did have a spooky habit of being able to read my mind: "Before you say anything, I can't ask Josh for help."

She's dropped her voice to a whisper. We've been joined at Karl Marx's grave by an **elderly** man and woman. They look totally innocent – he's carrying a guidebook and she's holding a thermos flask – but Olga is still staring at them **suspiciously**, as though they're possible spies. "Josh is the first person they'll try. **Ditto** Melissa," she hisses.

They? Who are *they*? I wonder. Then Olga smiles. "But you and me, Hausmann – well, we were never exactly close, were we? So no one would ever *dream* that I might turn to you for help." She hesitates for just a single **beat**: "And I seem to remember that your aunt has that flat in Fitzrovia, doesn't she? The one she doesn't use very often."

"Oh no," I say, "now wait a moment …"

Olga's face **crumples**. I know what's coming: she's going to cry, of course. Olga crying is quite something, actually: even if you had had an artificial heart **fitted**, one made out of Kryptonite or platinum or something, the sight of Olga crying would still melt it. I don't have an artificial heart made of Kryptonite.

I look at Olga again. My response *should* be just to ignore her now, as she stands there with her **trembling** lip and big baby bunny eyes. She's *soooo* manipulative! Time to apply the old Friendship Test: would this person help *me* if I were in trouble?

It's very simple. If Olga were in my shoes and I were the

+++ elderly – älter +++ suspicious – argwöhnisch +++ ditto – ebenso +++ beat – *hier:* Pulsschlag +++ to crumple – *hier:* sich verziehen +++ to fit – einsetzen +++ to tremble – zittern +++

one being **chased** by my crazy dad, she'd simply shout to him: *Emily went that way*! Which is why I don't *totally* understand why I find myself saying, "Well, I'll talk to Nora …"

"Great," says Olga quickly. She instantly "cancels" her tears, I notice. "We can stop by where I've been staying and pick up my stuff and then go straight over to her place, OK?"

I think for a second. I suppose that *might* be alright. Nora's in Nottingham, after all, and won't be back until tomorrow at the earliest. I have a key and permission to use the flat as I need. One night can't hurt. Can it? But I know Olga. I have to try and cover myself a bit, too.

The deal I make with Olga – we actually shake hands in front of Karl Marx – goes something like this: she can sleep at Nora's flat tonight. Then we'll ask Nora when she gets back if Olga can stay a bit longer. Olga is to be totally honest with Nora about the possible danger she's in but is *not* allowed to put any emotional pressure on her. No Tears Allowed. If Nora agrees, then Olga can stay in cosy Fitzrovia while Nora risks her life in the Causcasus. And after that, well, I'm hoping there isn't an *after that*. Surely Olga will have sorted herself out by then.

There's one more condition: I'm allowed to tell Melissa everything that's happened today. Melissa knows, apparently, that Olga's left Florida but doesn't actually know for certain that she's in London. Olga isn't enthusiastic about telling her – *it's too dangerous*, she says. I notice, of

+++ to chase – jagen +++

course, that she's not worried about things being dangerous for *me.* But it's obvious that Olga won't be able to **resist** seeing Josh – who doesn't know that she's in London yet either – and I don't want any more secrets in the dorm.

Olga frowns. "I've no idea how to tell Joshie I'm here. Dad will have anyone who loved me followed. And he hates Josh. He might even be able to get hold of Josh's phone records, even hack into his e-mail. Money buys you just about anything." She smiles one of her **dazzling** smiles. "But maybe you can carry messages between us or something?"

Oh, yes, great. I think. I have the definite feeling that Olga would happily let me walk through a minefield. Remind me why I'm helping her?

+++ to resist – widerstehen +++ dazzling – umwerfend +++

Trust No One

I go with Olga to the youth hostel in Piccadilly where she's been staying since she fled from Florida. She tells me over and over again on the tube how *awful* the place is but, of course, when we get there I see that it's actually really nice. It's obviously the first time in Olga's life that she hasn't stayed in a 25-star hotel. She's pleased with herself: "They'd never think of looking for me in a *youth hostel!*"

I wait downstairs while Olga gets her stuff. I'm half-expecting her to be followed by 87 sweating **porters** bearing the 900 Vuitton suitcases that she always had with her at school but when she reappears she only actually has a small black rucksack with her. It's strange to see her carrying it herself.

Olga treats us to a taxi to Fitzrovia. I notice she stares very hard at the taxi driver before she gets in. *Trust no one* seems to be her new *Lebensmotto*. It probably always was.

When we pull up outside Nora's flat, I feel a bit weird – like a murderer returning to the *Tatort*. I almost feel like

+++ porter – Kofferträger +++

Nora's door should be **sealed** with that tape the police use to close off crime scenes. The scene of the love crime!

Once inside, I manage to show Olga where everything is without opening my mouth. I get sheets and blankets and a pillow out of Nora's airing cupboard so Olga can sleep on the sofa. I show her how the TV works. I show her how to double lock the door. Then I turn to leave and as I do so, Olga actually shows me the first sign of **gratitude** that I've had from her. She kisses me softly on the cheek and says, "Thanks." And funnily enough, that makes it all almost worth it.

I rush back to school. I'm hopelessly late, of course. I promised Miss Shaw that I wouldn't be long and I've been *hours*. I feel nervous and guilty as I report back to her at around 7.30 pm. I write: *sorry miss got delayed* on my Kitty notebook. and hold it out to her, smiling as innocently as I can.

Miss Shaw just smiles back, luckily, and says lightly, "Well, just as long as you didn't talk to any strangers!" I nod. Well, Olga's not a stranger. She's just *strange*. Or at least her life is.

It's eight o'clock by the time I get back to the dorm. Melissa, Sadie and Becks are all there, playing silent Monopoly on the floor. It's obviously been a fun game: they all look like they've been quietly laughing their heads off.

They interrupt the game to ask me where I've been. Or, more accurately, for Becks to write down in massive let-

+++ to seal – versiegeln +++ gratitude – Dankbarkeit +++

ters on an A4 pad: YOU BETTER NOT HAVE TALKED OR SADIE WILL KILL YOU!!!

I smile and shake my head. I'm lying for a good cause, though, so that makes it OK. Really.

I'm dying to "talk" to Melissa, of course, but don't want to risk Becks and Sadie's lives by "saying" anything in front of them. The sponsored silence is the perfect opportunity, actually, because it means I can pass Melissa notes to tell her what happened with Olga. We're supposed to be silent until midnight. So, after Sadie has **bankrupted** Becks and Melissa in Monopoly, and it's game over and we're all in bed, I lean over and slip a piece of paper to Melissa: *You'll never guess who I just met?*

Melissa gives me a look. The look tells me that no, she doesn't actually *know* who it was but that she probably can guess. I write another note: *She says hello, hair's not blonde any more, it's brown.*

Melissa raises her eyebrows. She leans over and grabs my notepad and scribbles furiously: *Where on earth is she staying? Is she safe?*

My turn again: *She's OK. She's staying with the woman who broke Miss Bardwell's heart.*

It's not like I really think that whoever might come after Olga will go through the bins outside Chalk Farm and read our correspondence but still, I do feel too scared to write down: *She's at Nora's.* I notice that Sadie is now looking suspiciously at us. She **coughs** and holds up a piece of paper: *What on earth are you two talking about?* And I

+++ to bankrupt s.o. – jmdn. in den Ruin treiben +++
to cough – husten +++

quickly "reply": *Just about how much fun sponsored silence was!* and Sadie grins broadly and promptly falls asleep.

Melissa, meanwhile, is impatiently waiting for more information. She got the reference to Nora kissing Mr Michaels, Miss Bardwell's ex-fiancé, at the Christmas party: *Can I see her*? is the next thing she writes.

I shrug my shoulders. *I don't know. She's really paranoid about being followed.*

Did you see anyone follow her? – No. – Can I tell Josh yet? – No.

And so it goes on. Note tennis. Melissa and me use an entire Amazonian rainforest's worth of paper to **convey**

+++ to convey – übermitteln +++

our messages until finally we join Sadie and Becks in the land of nod, falling asleep on our note covered beds.

The first thing everyone does when they wake up the next day is to talk LOUDLY at each other. "I must call my mum!" booms Becks. She's shouting even more than usual, as though she's forgotten how to work the volume control on her voice. "MUM WON'T BELIEVE IT!"

Sadie is too excited for words, ironically, and is dressed before any of us. "I need to work out exactly how much money we've made," she says. I watch her putting on her prefect's blazer – it has gold **braid** round its burgundy edges – and feel really proud of Sadie again.

You can hear girls shouting all along the corridors, about how brilliantly funny the sponsored silence was yesterday and how proud they are that they managed to keep their mouths shut for a whole day! Melissa is the only one who's not yelling and high fiving. I can tell that she's worried about Olga. She's normally always the first one of us to make it down to breakfast but today she waits behind so that we can go down together. "When are you going to see her next?" she mutters, as we walk down the stairs behind Becks and Sadie.

Looking briefly around for hidden microphones, I tell Melissa quickly, "The heartbreaker gets back today and I have to ask her if it's OK if the brunette stays." The brunette – officially our new codename for Olga. It's all a bit cryptic.

+++ braid – Borte +++

"I'm definitely coming with you," says Melissa in a voice that I know it's not even worth *trying* to argue with. "We can go separately if you like, I'll meet you there but I really need to see *the brunette*."

Oh God! Nora's place will be **packed**! I try to warn Nora by text that Olga, Melissa and me will be at the flat tonight but I don't get a reply. Oh well. Nora's really sociable. She'll be happy to see us! Yeah! So that evening I leave school an hour before Melissa does, stopping off at a supermarket on the way to Nora's to make a few impulse **purchases** in case Olga's hungry: a frozen pizza, a big packet of crisps and some grapes.

When I ring the buzzer, "the brunette" lets me in without saying anything over the entry phone. She opens the door to the flat very slowly and looks at me for a moment from behind Nora's security chain. When Olga finally decides to let me in, I can see at once that she looks better than she did yesterday. "I slept really well," she tells me cheerfully. "I feel safe here." Not *that* safe – she immediately puts the security chain back on after me, I notice. And when the buzzer sounds a couple of minutes later, her face falls in horror. "That'll be Melissa," I say quickly and Olga's shocked but happy, too.

She's even happier when Melissa does burst in, pushing past me and throwing her arms around Olga. There are lots of *darlings* and *I love yous* and *how I've missed yous* and it's actually all a bit much for me. I feel like a

+++ packed – überfüllt +++
purchase – Einkauf +++

total **spare wheel**. I take the food I bought into the kitchen and decide to heat up the pizza. If the girls aren't hungry and I have to eat it all, then I have to eat it all. I'm ready to make that **sacrifice**.

I continue to hide from all the super girly emotion in the kitchen for a while after I've put the pizza in the oven. I try not to listen in but it's a small flat. Olga's busily telling Melissa everything – and I mean *everything* – that happened with Taki. So I'm just standing there, whistling and counting the cheese bubbles when I hear the sound of someone trying to open the door. My heart **leaps**. The security chain is on, of course, so they can't manage.

I run out again into the living room, where Olga is practically hiding under the sofa and Melissa is looking at me with terrified eyes. "It's Nora," I say firmly, praying that it *is* an attractive blonde woman in a Prada coat and not someone called Boris carrying an axe. I take the chain off the door and open it. It *is* Nora, of course. And Chris.

+++ spare wheel – Ersatzrad +++ sacrifice – Opfer +++ to leap – hüpfen +++

The Sofa of Love

I think I mentioned before that my heart leapt when I heard the key in the door. Now it's like my heart is at some theme park for body organs: it trampolines, it goes on the **roller coaster** and ends up on the carousel. Chris! He's carrying a very heavy looking box and looks just as shocked to see me as I am to see him. Which is very shocked indeed.

Oh, I can't stand it! I run at Nora and hug her. With my face buried in her coat, I mumble, "I tried to call you."

I feel Nora laugh against my head. "Oh, my phone was stolen somewhere. Chris and me weren't exactly in the nicest part of town." Of course, the riots! I've sort of been following the news but as usual my own life has been such a **blooming** riot that I forgot about them a bit.

I don't want to pull away from Nora. She smells so nice and I feel safe here, hiding my face from Chris. I'm so sure that my head is a little *rote beete* with long brown hair. I'm confused. On the one hand, it's like the best thing in the world to see Chris. On the other hand, I wanted to meet him again when I was wearing something half-way cool

+++ roller coaster – Achterbahn +++ blooming – *hier:* verteufelt +++

or when I'd rehearsed a couple of casual but funny things to say. Instead, I'm standing here in my uniform, hanging on to my aunt like I'm five or something. Brilliant.

Nora's now saying, "I wasn't expecting to see you and your friends! How nice!" And I know that that's my **cue** to explain what Melissa and Olga are doing here but I can't seem to get any words out. It's like the sponsored silence all over again.

I have to come out from my cover. I have to introduce them all. I cough, stare at my feet and begin, "Chris, Melissa. Melissa, Chris." Then I realise that everyone here actually sort of knows each other already. Some of us more intimately than others, of course. Melissa and Chris met during the strike and Nora was at that weird Christmas party last year when Olga announced that she was leaving Chalk Farm school. Olga is now making her way confidently over to Nora, to introduce herself "formally".

She shakes Nora's hand, then tells her, in her best little girl voice, about how she's an old school friend of mine and that she's had a fight with her family. "I need a little bit of time for the **dust** to settle," she says in an adorable and helpless kind of way. I give Olga a look that I hope says, *No emotional **blackmail** remember*, and Olga just smiles at me. She knows it – Nora's a big-hearted soft target!

She's also an **exhausted** one. She's just let her long blonde hair down and is trying not to yawn as she listens

+++ cue – Stichwort +++ dust – Staub +++
to blackmail – erpressen +++ exhausted – erschöpft +++

to Olga. Poor thing: this is probably the last thing she wants, a flat full of neurotic teenage girls with crazy stories.

Nora can't stay standing any longer and falls back onto the sofa – yes, *that* sofa – and starts to rub her feet. Olga sits down next to her and then Melissa sits down next to *her*. That leaves only Chris and me standing **awkwardly** in the middle of the room. There's no way either of us are going near that sofa again! The sofa of love!!

I still haven't actually managed to look Chris in the eye. Those eyes, mmmm. **Yummy** eyes …

YIKES! Not so yummy burnt pizza! I suddenly remember the jumbo sized pepperoni has been in the oven far too long and I run like a **lunatic** into the kitchen. In a funny way, I'm actually quite relieved that I've ruined our dinner, as at least that gives me a genuine excuse to get away from Chris.

As I open the oven door, smoke comes out. Not a good sign, I once read in a cook book. I try to find something to lift the tray out – a **tea towel** or an oven glove – when suddenly a voice says, "Are you looking for this?"

Chris is standing right behind me, holding an old tea towel with a picture of a lion on it. This is one of the things I love about Nora's place, other than the fact it's a) empty a lot and b) I have the key for it: absolutely everything in her flat can tell a story, even the tea towels. She got this in Tanzania, I remember, for no very good reason.

+++ awkward – unbeholfen +++ yummy – lecker +++
lunatic – Verrückte/r +++ tea towel – Geschirrtuch +++

So there Chris is, holding out the Tanzanian tea towel with the lion's face sort of smiling at me. "You need this? Or can I get the tray out for you?" And, without actually waiting for an answer, he pushes past me gently, goes over to the oven, lifts the tray out and places it on the top of the cooker. For a moment we both stare at the pizza, like two archaeologists trying to identify what exactly it is we've dug up.

"You could **scrape off** the dark bits," says Chris carefully.

I laugh. I can't help it. I laugh. If you scraped off the dark bits you'd be left with air: the whole pizza is **charcoal.** I feel my whole body relax. It's great – we can laugh about something. We can be *normal.* Chris smiles. He looks relieved, too. He whips out his phone with his hairy teenwolf hands. "Shall I order us all a pizza? Nora and me are starving, too."

So that's how I find myself sharing a super delicious, 16 inch (about 30 cm, I'm in Britain!) Vegetarian pizza with Nora, Melissa, Olga and Chris. For such a strange mix of people, the atmosphere is surprisingly relaxed. Nora chats to Olga about Russia and Melissa and Chris rerun the strike again. Me, I don't say very much. I'm just happy to be **nibbling** on bits of cheese and artichoke near Chris and not to have things be too weird.

Melissa asks Nora shyly how she's feeling "after what

+++ to scrape off – abkratzen +++ charcoal – Holzkohle +++ to nibble – knabbern +++

happened with Miss Bardwell". Nora sighs. "Oh, I'm fine. It was nothing really. I actually feel a bit bad for Connie, I mean, Miss Bardwell. Chalk Farm was her life. What on earth will she do now?"

No one answers, though I notice that Chris makes his "I'm a serious investigative journalist" face, as if to indicate that he *could* find out for us. Nora seems keen to change the subject and she hastily asks Olga about school. "Oh, I **graduated** already! I have an American High School Diploma. A whole year early!" She rolls her eyes. "It was *ridiculously* easy."

Melissa and Olga have been sitting next to each other,

+++ to graduate – den Schulabschluss machen +++

pretending to eat their bits of pizza and holding hands the whole time. My relationships with boys have been strange, I'll give you that, but nowhere *near* as strange as their friendship is. I just don't get it – they "split up" over Olga lying to Melissa about Josh but now it seems like they are back on again. **Go figure.**

Melissa looks totally exhausted by all the emotion and drama, actually. She's yawning and that makes me wonder how late it actually is. I look at my watch. *9.41.* **Curfew** is at ten! The school's not far from here but we don't have time to take the tube now. We'll have to get a taxi if we're going to make it. Or maybe Nora would **give us a lift**. I can't ask her, I decide: she's far too tired.

I mutter urgently, "We have to go," and Melissa also looks guiltily at her watch and **squeals**. "Oh Emily! I *totally* forgot! Can you ring for a taxi?"

"I'll take you both back to school," says Chris quietly. "I should be going, too." He stands up, wiping his fingers on a serviette.

"Chris, you're a star!" laughs Nora. She smiles at us, rather proudly, actually. "Chris only passed his test three months ago but he's a great driver. We took his car up to Nottingham – mine is …"

"… dying," finishes Chris. "We really need to get you that **hybrid** you're always talking about! Go green!" He apologises quickly when he sees how sad Nora looks. She really does love her old car and she just can't bear to sell it.

+++ Go figure. – Stell dir vor. +++ curfew – Sperrstunde +++ to give s.b. a lift – jmdn. im Auto mitnehmen +++ to squeal – kreischen +++ hybrid – Hybridauto +++

Even though he's just told her to kill her car, Nora still manages to smile again at Chris. You can see how **fond** she is of him. All that surviving riots and stuff can really bring you together. It's nice, though I find myself sort of hoping they haven't become *too* close. I mean, Nora's more than twice Chris' age but she's hot. And I bet Chris is into older, intelligent women …

"Emily," says Olga suddenly in a sharp voice. "Earth to Emily? The clock is ticking." Ooh, Little Miss High School Diploma is really enjoying the fact that she doesn't have to rush back to school any more, I think.

Even if it is **annoying**, the sound of Olga's voice is still useful: it brings me crashing back down to Planet **Sanity**. What *on earth* was I thinking? That was madness! *Of course* there's nothing going on between Nora and Chris! He has a girlfriend, remember? He's not the **cheating** kind.

I quickly hug first Olga, then Nora, who gives me a funny look. She whispers to me, "Listen, I'll call you tomorrow. Olga can stay as long as she likes. You know that I'm going to Grozny this week …" She hesitates and hands me her own key. I think it's a kind of **bribe**. Nora knows I *hate* it when she goes to danger zones.

It's a tiny bit ironic, Chris making jokes about Nora's car, as his own set of wheels probably wasn't at this year's motor show either. It's a blue Nissan and not really cool – it's his dad's old one, he tells Melissa and me quickly. On

+++ to be fond of s.b./s.th. – jmdn./etw. mögen +++
annoying – lästig, nervig +++ sanity – Verstand, Vernunft +++
to cheat – betrügen +++ bribe – Schmiergeld +++

the other hand, cool ride or not, it is totally ***awesome*** that Chris can actually drive.

When we reach the little Nissan, I immediately try to get in the back seat but Melissa beats me to it. "Oh Emily, sit in the front and keep the driver company, won't you? I want to stretch out here. I'm *soooo* tired …"And with that she gets in, **uncurls** herself and her long legs, taking up all of the back seat. So that's settled it. I'm sitting next to Chris.

I get in the front, trying to act cool and like it's no big deal, even though my heart is thumping so hard that I'm surprised my school tie isn't moving up and down. I **fasten** my seatbelt. It's only a ten minute drive to school, I can stand it. I'll just ask Chris about the riots. He'll talk and talk about them and then we don't have to mention anything that happened on a certain sofa. We can't anyway, with Melissa around.

Chris **puts the car into gear** and off we go, with Melissa yawning noisily for the eight billionth time behind us. I wish I could say that I am unimpressed by the sight of Chris at the wheel but I'd be lying. He looks so relaxed, so amazing. *Ooh, concentrate on the scenery, Hausmann!* I stare hard out of the window, watching as we drive past the BT Tower, London's very own *Fernsehturm*, which is always sensational at night. It's all quite perfect, somehow. Driving round the city with a gorgeous guy. *Oh, no! Don't think fancying thoughts!*

+++ awesome – großartig +++ to uncurl – sich ausstrecken +++ to fasten – schließen +++ to put the car into gear – den Gang einlegen +++

I say loudly, "So tell me about Nottingham," and that's it, Chris is off. He talks and talks about the desperate living situations he saw on the housing estates there, how brutal some of the police had been. It sounds awful and I am, truly, honestly, moved by what he says.

"Did you see my story?" Chris then asks quietly. I nod. I don't want to say anything too *schmeichelhaft* but I manage to mumble: *Really well written.*

"Thanks," he says. He glances at me out of the corner of his eye and smiles. "Shall we switch the radio on? I want to catch the news in a few minutes." It's five to ten, I notice now, and we should just make it back to Chalk Farm school in time. Just.

Chris reaches for the **radio dial**, then frowns. "What's that funny noise?"

I listen. It's a gentle sort of motorboat engine noise? Hmm, there aren't exactly a lot of **marinas** in Camden. No, it's actually a snoring sound! I glance at the back seat – I'd almost forgotten Melissa was there. She's only half with us, of course: she's fallen asleep.

I burst out laughing. How could anyone – even a teenage girl – fall asleep that quickly! It's the shortest trip in the world! Round the corner! And it's totally strange for another reason: with Melissa off in Sleepybye Land, Chris and me are effectively alone together. Only for a few minutes, of course.

Chris laughs at Melissa, too, but I can tell he's also

+++ radio dial – Sendersuche +++ marina – Jachthafen +++

wondering if it's safe to discuss what happened on the sofa of love. He hesitates and then says quietly, "You got my e-mail then?"

I look back at Melissa. She wouldn't fake being asleep, she's too honest. She's not Cyclops or Olga or … *me.*

"Yes, I got it," I mumble in the direction of my passenger's window. Then I pause. "Emm, thanks." I add, a bit lamely.

Chris sighs. "Well, there's absolutely nothing to thank me for, that's for sure. I'm sorry, Emily, I should have been more honest with you. I should have stopped things right away."

Ooh, *peinlich*! I don't really want to hear this, I realise, but as we haven't quite yet reached the school and I don't want to die young by throwing myself out of a moving car, I suppose I'll have to.

Chris wants to tell me everything, it seems. Nightmare. "I've been with Antonia for two years now. She's still back in Newcastle but she's about to start university here. She's the same age as me …"

Antonia. University. **Daggers** in my heart. Does Chris actually think that I want to hear this stuff? I'm actually wishing that Melissa would wake up so I wouldn't have to listen to any more of it. *Antonia. Nobel prize for Physics. Miss North East England. Blah Blah.* Whatever. I'm sure she's *perfect.*

Finally – we're actually safely back at school! I've never been so happy to see Chalk Farm in all my life! We pull

+++ dagger – Dolch +++

into the drive and Chris parks the car right in front of the main door. Then he switches the engine off and we sit in silence for a moment. Melissa is, amazingly, still dead to the world, still snoring gently. She'd be *sooo* embarrassed if she knew!

Chris is staring ahead in silence and I realise it's my turn to say something. To try and save what I can of my pride. Slowly, I manage to get out the words, "It's cool, Chris. No biggie. These things happen."

These things happen. Oh yeah, like all the time! I've kissed two other boys in my life and here I am sounding like I'm Paris Hilton or something.

Chris nods, still staring at the door to the school and not me. Then he says quietly, "I know the trying to be friends thing was a bit cheesy but I really enjoy working with you. This doesn't have to **spoil** things, does it?"

Hmm. I still have some pretty horrible memories of the times I've "tried to be friends" with boys in the past. Firstly with Sam, of course, when we sort of broke up for a while. That didn't work – we found that we couldn't actually manage to keep things platonic. Then there was Sebastian Junger, the boy I thought I fancied from Berlin. We were supposed to be friends, too, but he hasn't contacted me *once* since that disastrous trip he made to see me in spring here when I rejected him. Some friend he **turned out** to be.

I'm just wondering how to explain this to Chris when the ten o'clock news comes on the radio and Chris im-

+++ to spoil – verderben +++ to turn out – (sich) herausstellen +++

mediately says, "Sorry, you don't mind if I hear this, do you?"

The fact that it's the ten o'clock news means, naturally, that it's ten o'clock and I should wake Melissa up and get out of the car and into school, of course. The curfew is strict. I even heard the school call the police automatically if you're later than 10.30. But somehow Chris' interest in the news is totally **infectious** and I decide that 10.04 is *probably* OK.

They're now discussing the riots in Nottingham: *Tonight things are more peaceful on the streets here …* Chris nods, then shakes his head, then frowns. I could watch his face all night, it's so expressive.

Then suddenly a ghostly voice from the back seat says, "Is it really after ten? Emily, we'd better get inside pronto!" Melissa's awake finally and I turn to see her rubbing her eyes. She looks like Bambi in a uniform: big eyed, sweet and confused. She's right, of course, and so we say a hasty goodnight to Chris, **pile out** of the car and rush up the steps, like two Cinderellas escaping from a Nissan that's about to turn into a **pumpkin**.

+++ infectious – ansteckend +++
to pile out – sich hinausdrängen +++
pumpkin – Kürbis +++

The Evil 4 x 4

Well, I've done it at least. I've seen Chris **properly** and it was more relaxed and normal than I dared to imagine it would be. I can now carry on working at *The Sentinel* without **fainting** every time I go anywhere near him. That's a positive. The negative is that I really can't stop thinking about Chris. His face as he listened to the news, for instance. He genuinely cares about people in trouble. He's got the same quality that Nora has: he's a **humanitarian**.

I talk to Nora later that day, a **farewell** call before she leaves for Chechnya. It seems like Olga has been telling her something about the "danger" she's in. Nora's worried. "Honestly, if it's all as dangerous as she says it is, it might be better if she got police protection or something. Watch your back. I've had a word with Chris and he'll help you out if you need it. I'm going to text you his mobile number."

Ha! Someone who's off to the most **perilous** area in the world is telling me to watch my back! Hilarious! I know

+++ 4 x 4 – Auto mit Allradantrieb, Geländewagen +++
properly – richtig +++ to faint – ohnmächtig werden +++
humanitarian – Menschenfreund/in +++ farewell – Abschied
+++ perilous – gefährlich +++

what I think is less dangerous – looking after Olga or taking pictures in Grozny.

And actually, I've been wondering a bit about Olga's stories. She always was a bit of a drama queen. Maybe she's just **making** all this stuff about being followed **up**. Maybe she's just looking for attention or for someone to be her slave. Someone like *me*, of course. She actually managed to get me to agree to talk to Josh for her earlier. Olga can't phone him, *obviously*, because she says that's too risky. Or would it just be too easy? Is she simply enjoying having me run around after her?

Just because Olga's left America doesn't mean that her father is chasing her. Maybe Taki dumped her or maybe she just had a normal teenage fight with her parents. Or maybe …

And then suddenly all the *maybes* stop. Suddenly I don't have any doubts at all that Olga's telling the truth.

My doubts about the danger Olga's in disappear at lunchtime the following day. That's when I'm on my stupid mission to find Josh and tell him that Olga's here and would like to meet him. It shouldn't be all that difficult to find Josh, of course. As Olga was kind enough to **point out**, Josh is only "across the street". He's a pupil at St Dougan's Boys' School which is directly opposite our school. "I hear you're *really familiar* with the place," Olga had said, **cattily**. **What a cheek!** I've only been out with two of the boys there. Two!

+++ to make s.th. up – etw. erfinden +++ to point out – betonen +++ catty – boshaft +++ What a cheek! – So eine Frechheit! +++

Melissa has **tipped me off** to where Josh eats lunch – a salad and juice bar, apparently – so I slip out of class as fast as I can and wait outside our school gates. St Dougan's have their lunch break when we do and I'm just in time to see the first boys coming out of their school.

I wait and wait. And as I'm waiting and waiting, I notice a car with blacked out windows also waiting and waiting. You couldn't really miss the car: it's parked right next to the St Dougan's gates and it's a huge and expensive looking, cream coloured 4 x 4. At first I'm not too worried about it. It could belong to some rich boy's parents, I suppose.

+++ to tip s.b. off – jmdm. einen Tipp geben +++

I think for a moment. St Dougan's is a boarding school, though, like ours, and you don't often see parents waiting in cars outside the school on a Wednesday. Hmm. It couldn't be, could it? I keep my eyes on the car, waiting for someone to get out or for it to move on but it stays right where it is. And there's no sign of life from within.

There is now a sign of Josh-shaped life coming out of the St Dougan's gates with two other boys. I haven't seen Josh for ages and he seems to have grown about a metre and half since I last laid eyes on him. I'd forgotten what a handsome guy he is, well built, muscular, a rugby god – if you like that kind of thing. Which I don't, obviously. I seem to have a bit of thing about sort of **nerds**, I'm noticing. Boys who are into boring stuff like music or computers or ***current affairs***.

I'm just about to go over to Josh and wondering if a) he'll remember who I am and b) how on earth I'm going to get him on his own to tell him about Olga when I notice that the back window of the 4 x 4 has been **wound down**. A face pops out **cautiously**: a man wearing sunglasses. Then the front window slides down and another face appears, a dark haired, **tanned** handsome one. I recognise the face at once. It's Olga's Uncle Dimitri, who came with her to the Kensington Christmas party and took her back to America!

I **gasp**. I've stopped dead in my tracks. One of the men

+++ nerd – Langweiler/in +++ current affairs – (politisches) Tagesgeschehen +++ to wind down – herunterdrehen +++ cautious – vorsichtig +++ tanned – gebräunt +++ to gasp – nach Luft schnappen +++

in the car, the one with sunglasses who isn't Uncle Dimitri, is now calling out to Josh! *By name. They know who Josh is. Olga was totally right.* Josh looks surprised but goes over to him.

I want to scream out STOP! STAY AWAY FROM THE 4 x 4! But I don't. I'm frozen with fear. I can hardly bear to watch. It's incredible! Josh might be kidnapped in broad daylight. And what on earth would I do to stop it? Jump on top of the **windscreen** like they do in films? I think not.

The man who called to Josh has stayed in the car and is now talking to him through his open window. I'm relieved to see that Josh's friends are still there, standing behind him, whispering and looking curious. I'd hate to see Josh facing up to these guys by himself.

Josh seems totally **stunned** and confused: he shakes his head, then shrugs his shoulders. Thank goodness he *really* doesn't know anything about Olga! It should be obvious to anyone that he's telling the truth. I hope.

I hang back, still on the other side of the road, and still unable to take my eyes off the scene in front of me. I have my fingers pressed tightly around my mobile, ready to call the police if I have to. Yes, that's what I'd do if anyone grabbed Josh, I'd scream for help, call the police, copy down the registration number of the car. In Germany I'd know if the car had come from Bremen or Hanover or whatever, but here in Britain all you can tell is the age of the car.

+++ windscreen – Windschutzscheibe +++
stunned – verblüfft +++

The conversation seems to be finishing. Josh is shrugging his shoulders again and is now walking away from the car. I wait, holding my breath, to see if anyone is going to get out of the car and follow him. No one does. But the car hasn't driven away yet either.

Instead, I notice that the man in the sunglasses is **craning** his head out of his window to look over at our school. More precisely, he's now looking at me … looking at him! Yikes. I need to act natural fast. I need to seem like I was just standing here waiting for someone. Waiting for …

Cyclops! With her stupid friend Laurie. Unfortunately, they're the first people to walk past me that I recognise. I'm just so hopelessly happy that I have someone I can pretend to have been waiting for. So I yell, "*Amanda!*" Like we were long lost sisters or something. She glares at me suspiciously. "What on earth do *you* want, Hausmann?" Laurie, Cyclops' "friend" and gold medallist in the World's Smallest Brain Event, echoes, "Yes, what do *you* want, Haltmann?"

This is probably going to end in a horrible fight but I don't care. Better Amanda and Laurie than the Men in Black over there. I hesitate and then say, "Have you heard from Miss Bardwell?" I know, I know. *Provocative.* But for some reason I can't think of anything else to ask. And I am sort of curious. No one seems to have any idea where Miss Bardwell has gone. There are **rumours**, naturally: that she's back in the **monastery** in Japan she stayed at last term after she split up with Mr Michaels.

+++ to crane – strecken, recken +++ rumour – Gerücht +++ monastery – Kloster +++

For a split second, as Amanda looks ready to **go ballistic**, I think it would be less dangerous to face the entire Russian army. She's gone pink everywhere – in the face, the ears, the neck. Even her big eyeball.

"Do you actually think I would tell *you*?" she thunders. "*You* were the one who ruined her life, remember! Don't even *pretend* that you care about her!"

Amanda's shouting at me. Brilliant. A nice authentic *Zickenkrieg*! Olga's uncle and his **cronies** won't want a scene and they'll stay well away from us. Thank God Amanda doesn't know who they are – she'd **betray** me to them in a heartbeat.

"Oh, I just … hoped she was OK," I say lamely. The men, I'm pretty sure, have stopped staring at us. The window of the evil looking 4 x 4 has been wound up. And Josh is long gone, of course. He'll be sitting eating his **beetroot** and carrot salad and trying to make sense of what just happened by now. There's *no way* I'm going after him.

No, I'm just going to stand here and have the "hair-dryer in my face" experience that is Cyclops roaring at me. "I wouldn't tell you anything, no way," Amanda says fiercely. "You just want to laugh at how she's fallen!"

Well, yes, I would love to, I think but I shake my head. What I'd love to do more than anything is get away from Amanda and have some lunch in peace. But I can't, of course. Now I've opened Pandora's box, I'm going to have to sit here while the contents hit me in the face. On it goes,

+++ to go ballistic – ausrasten +++ crony – Kumpan +++
to betray – verraten +++ beetroot – Rote Bete +++

on and on. Cyclops tells me that I'm a home-**wrecker**, a job-wrecker, a school-wrecker, a life-wrecker – basically I'm a bit of a wrecker!

At least I'm still a wrecker with a **pulse**.

+++ ...wrecker – ...verderber/in +++ pulse – Pulsschlag +++

Electro Pop

No way I can keep this to myself! I finally escape from Hurricane Cyclops and race back inside to the school cafeteria, where I've a good idea that I'll find Melissa. The food in the cafeteria is terrible – **beef olives** anyone? – and I've a **sneaky** feeling that Melissa lunches here as part of a weird sort of diet. There's no chance of getting fat if you "eat" our school food, after all.

I'm right – Melissa's sitting at her usual table with Becks. I rush over to them. As luck would have it, I've still got my Hello Kitty notepad and pen in my blazer pocket and once I've caught my breath, I write Melissa a quick note – JUST SEEN SOME BIG RUSSIANS TALKING TO JOSH! Melissa gasps and gets up immediately from the table, leaving behind a confused Becks.

Melissa and me head speedily for the nearest toilets where I tell her in whispers exactly what I just saw. Melissa looks quite faint. She can't speak and simply starts biting her nails frantically. We're still standing there, wondering at the drama and danger of it all, when

+++ beef olive – eine Art Roulade +++
sneaky – schleichend +++

Melissa's phone rings. She stares guiltily at her pocket. We're still not supposed to use our phone at lunch times but ever since the sponsored silence the rule seems to have been unofficially relaxed.

Melissa pulls out her phone and stares at it with an expression of panic. She flashes the display at me: JOSH.

"Just tell him you know nothing," I hiss. "*Nothing.*"

Nothing. That's exactly what I have to tell everyone else I know about what's going on. It's cruel and inhuman punishment, of course. I'm suddenly living the life of an international **spy**, full of danger and intrigue and romance and excitement. I'm kissing journalists. I'm hiding **fugitives**. But I'm not allowed to breathe a word of any of it.

I've got something else on tonight anyway. Kim's performing live in London's West End! Or at least her dance class is doing a show at the local **community centre**. Kim's going to Tango live with her boyfriend Jonathan and she's *totally nervous*. Maudie is to be her "make-up and wardrobe assistant" and I'm on photography duty.

And you know what? I'm just going to forget about Olga for one night and concentrate on being there for Kim and taking some nice photos. I should phone Olga to tell her what happened with Josh but I really can't face it. Olga'll *freak out* and then I just know that she'll guilt-trip me into going over there to comfort her. Not tonight. Tonight's Kim's night.

+++ spy – Spion/in +++ fugitive – Flüchtige/r +++ community centre – Gemeindezentrum +++

So that evening, Maudie, Kim and me go backstage to Kim's dressing room and help her get into a very kitschy red and green flamenco dress. Maudie puts Kim's make-up on and does a really good job of making her look like "Penelope Cruz", as Kim had **requested** (not easy as Kim is blonder than blonde). I take some "before" and "after" shots. Jonathan floats in from time to time, looking very Latino lover like, in a **low-cut** shirt and *very* tight trousers that make Maudie really *giggle.*

When we've finished making Kim look as hot and spicy as a **jalapeña** muffin, Maudie and me take our seats and the show begins. Unfortunately, Kim and Jonathan

+++ to request – erbitten +++ low-cut – tief ausgeschnitten +++ jalapeña – südamerikanische, scharfe Paprikaart +++

are dancing second from last so we have to sit through all the other acts, some of which are cute – little girls dressed up as rabbits! – and partly not so cute. There are a lot of *bad* hip hop dancers, for instance.

They're not as bad, however, as the last act before Kim and Jonathan, which is a truly terrible expressive dance number by a woman who looks old enough to know better. She's dancing to "Total Eclipse of the Heart". Oh boy, she must be fit for her age because it goes on and on …

Kim asked me to take a photo of all the acts and as I raise my camera to shoot this woman, Maudie hisses, "Oh, don't take *her* picture! God, she's terrible! Why didn't anyone tell her? Doesn't she have friends? You'd tell me if I were that bad, wouldn't you?"

I laugh but, well, I remember that Maudie didn't respond too well recently when I did try and let her know what I thought she was doing wrong. But that's all behind us, of course. Maudie's now whispering to me about some amazing Swedish electronic music she's into. "I'll get you a copy," she hisses as the middle-aged dancer pretends to **stab** herself in the heart. "I'm *so* over guitar music right now. Electro synth pop, that's where it's at!"

Right, I say. *Wrong*, I'm thinking. Maudie's boyfriend Matt is, of course, the bassist in a guitar pop band. I hope that doesn't mean she's *over* him! The Kitty Gagarins are still cool, though naturally – in my own **humble** opinion – the fire has gone out of them a bit since my ex-boyfriend Sam left them.

+++ to stab – (er)stechen +++ humble – bescheiden +++

Right on cue, Maudie says quietly, "I'm trying to get Matt into electro pop a bit. I really think they need to update the band's sound. I mean, if they're really serious about **capturing** the zeitgeist …"

Wow, did Maudie really say zeitgeist? And wow again – as in *wow*, that sounds like a totally *bad* idea! Matt and the boys are guitar crazy. They'd rather swap their guitars for bongos and triangles than synthesisers, I suspect.

Hmm. I was hoping that Maudie had stopped being *quite* so controlling. She seems to have relaxed about Matt a bit – he's allowed out **occasionally** by himself at least – and I only hope she's not now going to be too possessive of his band's sound. I hope she's not going to turn into Yoko Ono or anything.

Maudie **pokes** me in the ribs. "What's going on with you? Any **gossip** for me?" The expressive dance woman now, fortunately, appears to be "dying". The audience applaud loudly.

I clap, too, and try to look vague. "Oh, nothing much. Business as usual." Yeah, right. Kissing journalists and hiding Russians. So very *business as usual.*

Finally it's time for Kim and Jonathan! Their number is pretty hot stuff somehow, all very Latin American dirty dancing. Kim even has a rose between her teeth! Maudie and me clap and howl ARRIBA! and OLÉ! and lots of silly things. It's fun. For an hour or two, I've now successfully managed to forget about a frightened Olga sitting in Fitz-

+++ to capture – erfassen +++ occasionally – gelegentlich +++
to poke – stoßen +++ gossip – Tratsch +++

rovia and a very lovely Chris leaning over his laptop somewhere with the perfect and beautiful Antonia bringing him a cup of **herbal tea**. Yes, indeed, all forgotten.

+++ herbal tea – Kräutertee +++

Gone Baby Gone

All forgotten until the next night. That's when it's time to go and see if Olga's still alive. It's dark by the time I leave school. It's not **pitch black** – London does actually have street lamps – but I still feel jumpy as I walk down the **creepy**, tree-lined drive towards the gates. And, oh lordy, actually I'm right to be so nervous because … there it is. The evil looking 4 x 4. Parked exactly where it was the other day. I should just ignore it and keep walking but I don't. I can't. I'm frozen. I'm a frozen chicken.

I don't actually know what to do. I try to think of all the brave people I know: Nora, Chris … *Chris.* I hesitate for all of 0.014^{th} of a second, then I get out my phone and I scroll down to the visiting card Nora sent me with Chris' number in it. I call him. I'm honestly terrified. And stuck. I feel like I have to get to Olga but I can't bring myself to walk past Uncle Dimitri's very, very big car.

Chris picks up on the second ring. He doesn't recognise the number, of course, and he sounds shocked to hear my voice. I tell him quickly what's happened and he doesn't hesitate. "I'm still at *The Sentinel* – I can be there

+++ pitch black – rabenschwarz +++ creepy – gruselig +++

in about 20 minutes. Go back inside and stay there. I'll pick you up."

I do as I'm told. It feels nothing like 20 minutes and very much like 20 years but finally I hear a car come up the drive. I'm sitting in the entrance hall of our school and at first I'm actually too scared to look out of the door. What if it's the 4 x 4?

I finally **pluck up** enough **courage** to peer outside the door and there it is – the blue Nissan! Thank all the stars above! I race out towards it and leap inside. I sit trembling for a second, without looking at Chris. This is too weird, naturally.

"Did you see the car?" I finally manage to say, breathlessly. Just for a horrible moment I'm afraid that the 4 x 4 will have gone and Chris will think this is some strange way of trying to get a date.

"I saw it," said Chris grimly. He's taking this very seriously which is nice but which also makes me even more afraid. "And you're sure?"

I tell him quickly about what happened with Josh. I tell him how I recognised Uncle Dimitri and how there can be no doubt that these men are looking for Olga. Chris nods a lot, then nods some more. He drums his fingers on the steering wheel, which reminds me of Sam. That's exactly what he used to do when he was thinking hard. Odd. Do I have a finger-drummer fetish, perhaps?

"I don't have any brilliant ideas at the moment," says Chris finally. "We've got to talk to Olga, that's clear. And

+++ to pluck up courage – Mut fassen +++

we need a plan. She has to get out of London. If these guys watch the school long enough, they'll work it out."

He looks at me. *What a look.* "And there's really no way that Olga could just talk to her father? Try and **resolve** this?"

I shrug my shoulders. I tell him what Olga has told me about her arranged marriage. Chris is shocked: "I mean, it's practically *slavery.*" I can almost see the words "GREAT STORY" written in neon across his **forehead** and I say quickly, "You can't write about this, you realise?"

Chris smiles. "I wouldn't do that. Plus, I quite fancy being able to celebrate my 18th birthday, you know."

So, that's how I find myself lying in the back of Chris' blue Nissan, looking up at the night sky and feeling like I did when I was a child, trying to sleep in the back seat on a long car trip. Chris doesn't speak as he drives but I now recognise a **high rise** at the far end of Chalk Farm Road. I know that we are well and truly past the 4 x 4. I'm just about to ask if I can sit up when Chris hisses, "Stay down! I think they really are following us."

I stay where I am, lying as stiff as a board. I try to **take my mind off things** by looking carefully at the contents of the back seat. Chris has luckily got quite a clean car. I'd hate to do this in my Auntie Nora's Citroën which always has mountains of **crumbs** and always, *always* smells of a dog that she borrowed about twelve years ago. **Yuck.**

+++ to resolve – (auf)lösen +++ forehead – Stirn +++ high rise – Hochhaus +++ to take one's mind off things – sich ablenken +++ crumb – Krümel +++ yuck – ekelhaft +++

Then I hear Chris mutter, "I'm going to try to lose them," and I think I must be dreaming. In fact, I end up closing my eyes. We've now officially crossed the line from "exciting scary" into "bad scary". We seem to be **weaving** around a bit.

Chris is really mumbling and I have to strain my ears to hear him at all now: "Emily, we can't go to Nora's place. I'm just going to head back to *The Sentinel*. They won't get past the front security gate there. We can wait for half an hour and see what happens. Phone Olga now and tell her what's going on – she'll be worried sick."

Still lying down, I manage to manipulate my phone out of my pocket and dial Nora's **landline** number. Olga picks up immediately. I explain what's happened and Olga squeals a little, like a puppy that's just been kicked. "It's fine," I tell her. "Honestly. Everything is going to be fine." Inside, I'm wondering desperately how on earth we are going to make this turn out well.

"Why do you sound like you're in a box?" Olga hisses, suspiciously.

"Because I'm lying down … oh **never mind**! We're going to try and lose them by going to *The Sentinel* first, OK? Just wait for us."

"Ring the buzzer three times so I know it's you," says Olga firmly. And then finally, quietly, she whispers, "And be careful."

She's just pleased it's not Melissa or Josh lying here

+++ to weave – (sich) schlängeln +++ landline – Festnetz +++ Never mind. – Egal. +++

having to *be careful*, of course. And actually, in a funny way, as I lie here staring at the back of Chris' neck – I've always had a bit of a thing about the back of boy's necks – so am I. At least if I die, I'll die with a brilliant view and a smile on my face.

Finally I realise that we must be at the gates of *The Sentinel* because Chris has wound down his car window and is showing his ID card and joking with the security guard. I hear Chris mutter, "Yeah, back again, I forgot my laptop."

We seem to be parking. Chris switches the engine off and says, "The coast is clear. You can sit up now." I **bolt** upright, too fast, and Chris laughs. I'd love to check what my hair is doing – I remember what Melissa's looked like after she'd been lying down here. But that would be silly and **vain**, right? I smooth it down a bit anyway and then get out of the car.

The Sentinel car park is very brightly lit, which makes me feel safe. Chris and me peer out into the darkness beyond the fence. "This would actually be the perfect place for Olga to live," I mutter and Chris laughs. But actually, I wasn't really joking. Maybe I could fix her up with Harry the security guard? That's the kind of guy she should be dating right now.

Chris and me behave totally suspiciously, of course. We go inside the newspaper building and hang out in the foyer for a while trying to decide whether we have enough

+++ to bolt – sausen +++ vain – eitel +++

time to grab a coffee. Even though we'd both love one, we finally decide it's not fair to keep Olga waiting any longer. "Phone her and tell her we're just leaving," says Chris. "Come on, they really didn't follow us. Let's just go."

So I phone Nora's flat. No one answers. I look at Chris in panic. I dial the number again. Chris is definitely one shade paler than he was a minute ago but he says reasonably calmly, "Maybe she's in the toilet? Or …"

"Let's not think about the *or*," I mutter. I feel sick to my stomach and the drive to Nora's place seems to last forever. Once we're finally there, I cross the street and I do as Olga told me and ring the bell three times. I wait and wait. Olga doesn't answer.

Chris and I exchange looks. We're both thinking the same thing, of course. I still have Nora's key so I whip that out and Chris and me **dash** upstairs. We get to the front door of the flat. It's closed and Chris murmurs, "No sign of a struggle."

My heart **skips** twelve beats or so as I turn the key and shout, "OLGA!" Actually, I don't so much open the door as **fling** it open, so hard in fact that I actually hit the telephone table right behind the door. It wobbles. So do my nerves. I know it already: Olga's gone.

I can honestly say that I've never been more frightened in my life when I realise that Olga's not in the flat. Chris and me search the whole place but she's definitely not here. The good news is that, as Chris said, there's no sign of a

+++ to dash – rasen +++ to skip – überspringen, *hier:* auslassen
+++ to fling – schleudern +++

fight. Olga's rucksack is still there. The only thing I can't see is her navy blue boyfriend blazer. But if she'd been kidnapped, they'd probably have let her take that anyway, wouldn't they? Her **pursuers** are family, after all.

Chris glances uneasily at the sofa of love and finally decides to sit on it. I **perch** myself very carefully on a chair opposite him. Chris watches me sit down and then sighs. "Listen, it looks like she left on her own. Maybe she's just went out to get something to eat?"

"She doesn't eat," I say flatly. But, of course, Chris is right. Olga's probably OK. She's a survivor, as Mr Benn once said. A couple of things do **bother** me: why didn't she leave a note? And she was so scared when I spoke to her before – would she really have dared to go out by herself? God, I wish Olga still had a mobile. She thinks it's too risky right now. How did people manage their lives without mobile phones?

Finally Chris says, "Let's give it an hour or so, then we should probably think about calling the police." We sit looking awkwardly at each other. I'm sure we can both hear it: the sound of *alarm bells* ringing! Déjà vu: we are in almost the same situation as we were before we kissed. A crisis has **occurred** and we're alone together. But there will be no kissing this time! We've established that Chris has a girlfriend. Antonia, remember?

So, if we're not going to kiss, how are we going to pass the time until Olga gets back … or doesn't? Putting the

+++ pursuer – Verfolger/in +++ to perch – sich hocken/setzen
+++ to bother – beunruhigen +++ to occur – passieren +++

TV on seems a bit strange and so does listening to music. Finally Chris says, "Shall we look at some of your aunt's photos?"

Fantastic. I'm so relieved to be able to actually do something that isn't kissing that I grab the first album I can lay my hands on. Unfortunately, it's one that just **happens to** have lots of pictures of me as a child, taken during one of Nora's visits to Berlin. Thank God it's not my baby pictures; there are no shots of me naked or anything. There *are* lots of me aged about three or four, looking quite cute, if I say so myself.

It's an easy, lovely way to pass the time. Chris and me talk and we talk and we talk as we look at the photos. It seems like each photo starts a different conversation. Nora's shots of Berlin: I tell Chris about life there, the architecture, the music scene. Shots of my parents – Chris and me swap stories about our families. His parents are actually – gasp – still happy together. They had him fairly late. "And they've sort of **semi-retired** to France now." Chris smiles. "I suppose they're what you used to call hippies. Mum **runs** watercolour painting courses and Dad, well, he's nearly 70. He does the garden, makes his own wine …"

Just then Chris's phone rings. It's lying on the coffee table in front of us and he looks at it and frowns, then leans over and presses "silent". I was very good and didn't try and look at the display but I know it was Antonia, I *know it.*

+++ to happen to (do s.th.) – zufällig (etw. tun) +++ semi-retired – halb zur Ruhe gesetzt +++ to run – *hier:* leiten +++

I can't worry about that for very long because at that very same moment my own phone rings. It's in my blazer pocket and I race over to Nora's coat stand to get it out and answer it. It must be news of some kind about Olga, surely. My hands are trembling. It's Melissa.

She sounds very **agitated** and comes straight to the point, "*Where are you*? Is everything alright? You do know it's after ten! You won't get in without having to ring the bell. Miss Shaw will kill you!"

Oh lord. *The time*. "I'm at Nora's waiting for Olga," I say slowly. I don't want to panic Melissa. But Melissa just says shortly, "Josh called me about 15 minutes ago.

+++ agitated – aufgeregt +++

Olga's still with him." She says this as though this should be obvious, that even the stupidest person would know this.

"*Still with Josh?*" I find myself shouting. "WE'VE BEEN WORRIED SICK! COULDN'T OLGA HAVE LEFT US A NOTE, EH? WE HAD ARRANGED TO MEET HERE!"

Melissa sighs. "Oh Emily, don't shout. It's not my fault! They told me she *did* leave you a note. She just panicked before, she said, and ended up calling Josh. They're still in some café and he's been trying to calm her down. They were wondering if they should ask Chris to come and pick Olga up and bring her back to Nora's."

I'm relieved and annoyed all at once. I'm totally glad that Olga isn't sitting **chained up** in some Learjet on her way back to Florida, of course. On the other hand, *what* note? And does Olga think Chris is some kind of taxi service? "I'll ask him if he can go and get her," I say **grumpily**. "But Melissa, it's all a mess. I've **dragged** Chris into something pretty risky. And now Josh is involved. What are we going to do with Olga? We can't keep going like this."

Melissa sighs, a great big heartfelt sigh. She agrees, it's clear, and it's not her fault, as she said. I hang up and tell Chris everything that's happened. "Oh man," he groans. "This is *totally* the last trip I'm making tonight!"

As we leave, Chris picks up a piece of paper lying near the door mat. It's Olga's note: GONE TO MEET JOSH.

+++ to chain up – anketten +++ grumpy – mürrisch +++ to drag – ziehen +++

WILL BE OK. DON'T WORRY. I must have knocked it off the telephone table when I came bursting in here before. I'm a one-girl disaster zone.

Grounded

Chris drives like a **bat** out of hell towards school. The good news is that when we arrive there there's no sign of the **sinister** 4 x 4. The bad news is that it's nearly 11 o'clock.

I want to say to Chris *You'd better not get out of the car.* Arriving late – bad. Arriving late with boy – extremely bad. But I can't get the words out fast enough and he's already out of the car and shaking my hand before I know it. His eyes are **glowing** a bit, I notice. He smiles. "It's been a crazy night, eh?" Then more shyly, "But I've enjoyed it. Really. I'll let you know how I get on with Olga. I'm going to put my thinking cap on about her. Good luck in there." He nods towards the school.

The main door is **indeed** *very* locked when I try to open it. I take a deep breath, say a few words to the Queen Mother and ring the bell for the first time ever. It's Miss Shaw who answers, looking grim faced. I smile weakly. I **get on** really well **with** Miss Shaw: she's no Miss Bardwell. She's reasonable. Usually.

+++ to be grounded – Hausarrest haben +++ bat – Fledermaus +++ sinister – unheimlich +++ to glow – glänzen, glühen +++ indeed – tatsächlich +++ to get on with s.b. – sich mit jmdm. verstehen +++

But it's very quickly clear, Miss Shaw *totally* isn't impressed. And, just as I feared, she *did* see Chris. So before I can try and get out my line about *having been busy helping a friend in need*, she says quickly, "And who was the young man who brought you here?"

Anything I tell her is going to sound really lame but I have a go anyway. "He works at the newspaper Miss …" and then I realise that I never *quite* got around to asking the school for permission to be at *The Sentinel*. I remember that Chalk Farm School was not really ***thrilled*** about Chris and Nora turning up to cover the strike. Oh brother. I'**m for it**, pure and simple.

+++ thrilled – begeistert +++ to be for it – erledigt sein +++

Miss Shaw is wearing a really nice sweatshirt, a sort of seventies-style one with a picture of an owl on it, paired with grey skinny jeans. She looks so young and cool but she's a teacher first and foremost, of course. She says **sternly**, "Emily, being out with boys after curfew – it's just not OK. We're responsible for your **welfare** while you're here. Your parents trust us and we take that trust very seriously."

She takes a deep breath. She isn't enjoying this. "Emily, I don't have any other choice. Unless there was some kind of emergency this evening ..." She pauses and raises an eyebrow. Oh, it's **pointless**! Where would I even begin? I can't tell her anything about Olga! She wouldn't even believe me if I did tell her, I realise sadly.

I say nothing, just **scuff** my feet for a second and Miss Shaw sighs again. She throws her hair back and says firmly, "There's an automatic **penalty** for missing curfew and that's – no going out in the evening for two weeks."

Olga is all I can think as I march miserably back up the stairs to the dorm. *Who's going to feed Olga?* Like she was a pet rabbit or something. Oh well, it will just have to be Melissa's turn for a while.

It's way after lights out when I reach 3B but as I come in, I can just about see that Melissa is still sitting up in bed in the dark. Her eyes are flashing. *Talk to me* they say!

But I don't want to talk to Melissa right now. My head feels like it has that giant 4 x 4 parked in it. I need to get

+++ stern – ernst, streng +++ welfare – Wohlergehen +++
pointless – zwecklos +++ to scuff – scharren +++
penalty – Strafe +++

to bed. And as I **stagger** towards it, I mutter Chris' words of wisdom to Melissa: "We have to get Olga out of London. *We have to.*"

It's no fun to be grounded but in an odd way I'm a *tiny* bit relieved that I don't have to worry about Olga for a while. Melissa will look after her, feeding her, emptying her cage, etc. At least I'm allowed out at weekends and can keep on going to *The Sentinel.* If I'm honest, being grounded at weekends would have hurt much more than during the week.

I've no sooner walked into *The Sentinel* on the following Saturday when Chris appears out of nowhere and grabs me. He looks a bit rough. He obviously hasn't **shaved** for a while and his face is losing the battle against his hair. "Come on," he murmurs. "Let's go to the breakout areas. I need to tell you something." He grabs me by the arm. My arm faints.

Once we're in the second floor breakout area – the spaces where journalists can relax a bit – Chris doesn't waste any time. I sit a bit awkwardly on one of the Fat Boys there and Chris flops down on one next to me, excitedly. "I spent a lot of time talking to Olga the other night after I picked her up. And we've actually put together a bit of an escape plan. Did you know that she's very **keen** to improve her watercolour skills? Or that she also fancies **polishing** her French?"

+++ to stagger – schwanken +++ to shave – sich rasieren +++
keen – scharf auf +++ to polish – aufpolieren +++

I stare at him. *Watercolour skills? French?* I'm a bit annoyed, frankly. Personally, if I were Olga, I'd quite fancy working on my "Staying Alive" and "Not Putting My Friends' Lives at Risk" skills. Olga's thinking about going to whatever they call the *Volkshochschule* here in Britain, while we run around being chased by men in black. Nice one.

Chris laughs. "We're going to send Olga on a little trip to the Limousin region – to my parents' place! It's really the best idea we could think of. She can get her head together and I'm sure no one would ever think to look for her there."

I stare at Chris like he'd just explained the theory of relativity to me. In **Farsi.** It's a brilliant solution, of course. But, well, won't it then just move all the danger onto Chris' parents? Chris shrugs. "Ach, they're tough. And you'd never find the place, trust me. It's right off the map. I only hope Olga doesn't get bored out there in the middle of nowhere. There aren't exactly a lot of designer boutiques."

He smiles, then quickly looks more serious again. "Olga's a wreck, did you notice? And my mum's great, she can build her back up. I spoke to them this morning and they're really into the idea of having her. Mum's a total feminist so when I told her that Olga was being forced into a marriage, she was all ready to fight for her."

If I hadn't already unsuccessfully kissed Chris and then discovered he had a girlfriend, I would kiss him again now. I manage to **splutter**, "Great. Just *great*."

+++ Farsi – persische Schriftsprache +++
to splutter – hervorsprudeln +++

Chris is really pleased with himself, you can tell. And then he finally does something I can't believe – he stretches over, flings his arms round me and gives me a hug. I feel my heart beating against his **chest** for a second. I can even feel his stubble on my face. Oh wow, this can't be happening again, can it?

No, it can't. That would be too sweet. Real life has a sourer taste than that. Chris looks at me carefully for a moment and then coughs. He has no intention of kissing me. The only girl he'll be kissing this weekend is Antonia. End of story.

Things happen next at a speed I can't quite believe. Before you can say, "**Das vidanya**, London," Olga is booked on a flight to Limoges for the following week and we're sort of trying to arrange a top secret trip to the airport. Chris has got Olga a seat on an evening flight and I'm still technically grounded then, of course. But not saying goodbye to Olga, not putting a **lid** on this, feels all wrong.

So I decide to go on my knees to Miss Shaw. It's also been bothering me that I still haven't told her about working at *The Sentinel* at weekends. I go to her office after classes are over one day and **confess** all about my work experience at the paper. Miss Shaw looks shocked. "But Emily, that's amazing! That's a totally fantastic chance for you! Why didn't you just tell the school?"

"I did," I say **glumly**. "But Miss Bardwell refused me

+++ chest – Brust +++ das vidanya (russisch) – Auf Wiedersehen +++ lid – Deckel +++ to confess – gestehen +++ glum – mürrisch +++

permission to go on Wednesdays and so I had to sneak off at weekends and do it."

Miss Shaw says nothing. She plays a little bit anxiously with a **paper clip** that she has sitting on her desk. She clearly doesn't want to say anything nasty about Miss Bardwell and she obviously can't think of anything to say that would be professional.

Finally she sighs, "Well, it's a *pity* that Miss Bardwell didn't allow it, of course. Perhaps she didn't fully understand what doors it would open for a young photographer like yourself to get some experience at a national newspaper."

Ooh! Here's my chance! "And Chris works there, too, Miss," I say quickly. "The boy I was with the other night. We really had been at the newspaper. There was an emergency story to cover."

Miss Shaw **squints** at me. She's not totally buying that, I can tell. "Hmm, I'm not sure I want to know what kind of emergency. Anyway, Emily, why didn't you just *tell* me this the other night?"

Because I'm stupid, I think. So my curfew is lifted. Hurrah! And here's where the story sort of ends. Or at least here's how I thought this chapter of my London life would end: I would put Olga on a plane to France and everything would officially calm down again. I would go to *The Sentinel* and work really hard, trying to master computers and digital transfer technology and fascinat-

+++ paper clip – Büroklammer +++
to squint – schielen +++

ing things like that. I would continue to have a friendly relationship with Chris and we would slowly come to forget what happened that crazy day on the sofa of love. Perhaps I would even get to meet Antonia and be totally normal with her. We'd go shopping together, for example. **Hang out**.

I would go back to being the girl who listens to exciting stories about everyone else's love lives. Kim and Jonathan would tango off into the sunset. Maudie would become the Kitty Gagarin's new manager and get them a record deal. Sadie would become the boss of UNESCO or something. Cyclops would leave to join the new Super Bitch Academy that Miss Bardwell is probably founding in Peru or somewhere right now. Me personally, I would have officially the world's most boring life. The End. But that's not, actually, what happened next. Not at all.

+++ to hang out – rumhängen +++

Au Revoir Olga

It's *too weird.* At first things did go more or less as I **predicted** they would. I call Chris right after I've seen Miss Shaw and tell him I've been given an early release for good behaviour! I can go to the ball – or the airport. Just in time, too, Olga's flight is tonight.

We arrange to meet at Nora's. Chris has been there already today to see Olga: "And man, she's even *more* paranoid than ever. She's just terrified they'll catch us on the way or at the airport. She even wants us to take Nora's car because she's scared that her 'friends' might recognise mine. And no Josh or Melissa. They'll meet up in France later when ..."

"... the dust has settled," I finish. Olga loves that expression.

"Do you think it's really alright to drive Nora's car?" Chris says **doubtfully**. "Am I even ***insured*** to drive it?"

I have no idea. "I can try and e-mail her to ask," I say but, actually, I know I won't get a reply in time. Nora does

+++ to predict – vorhersagen +++ doubtful – zweifelnd +++ insured – versichert +++

occasionally check her mails but I don't think Grozny is exactly full of Internet cafés. I think it *sort of* is OK if we take the Citroën. "If you crash it, I suppose that might mean Nora finally gets a new car," I say brightly.

"Great," says Chris glumly. "That makes me feel a *whole lot* better."

Olga's flight is at nine and she wants to leave Fitzrovia by six so I come straight out of "homework club" and jump straight into the tube. Chris is already at the flat when I arrive there and looks **tense**. Olga is plainly super nervous: she snaps at me when I walk in. "Where have you been? We have to get going."

+++ tense – angespannt +++

She's wearing a baseball cap and sunglasses again. It's an outfit which screams to me I AM ON THE RUN, but I suppose she could be anyone. Anyone famous anyway.

Olga has her little rucksack already packed and I take Nora's car key down from the **hook** above the telephone table where it always hangs. Then I say a quick prayer that Nora *won't actually* mind and that Chris *won't actually* crash the car and we all try to walk as calmly as we can to Nora's **groovy maroon** Citroën.

Olga gets in first. "PHEW!" she says as she sits in the back and I take my "usual" co-driver's seat. "This car *stinks*." She holds her nose. "Ooh, I'm not sure what's worse – Uncle Dimitri or that smell!"

It's the first joke she's made in ages and Chris and me laugh enthusiastically. But Olga's face quickly clouds again and she hisses, "*Drive*." Chris sighs and then **fiddles** with the **gear stick**: "Boy, it's stiff!" He turns the **ignition** key a few times before the engine finally gives a weak cough. "It's cold," says Chris. He looks worried. I love it when he looks worried. I love the way his eyebrows frame his face when he frowns.

Finally the Citroën seems to gather enough energy and we **jolt** off towards Stansted Airport. It's quite far out of town and it's a reasonably long drive. Nobody says much

+++ hook – Haken +++ groovy – schick +++
maroon – kastanienbraun +++ to fiddle –
hier: fummeln +++
gear stick – Gangschaltung +++
ignition – Zündung +++to jolt – holpern +++

on the way. Chris is clearly concentrating on driving a car built 20 years before he was born and Olga and me, well what to say? She's still very, very tense. She even snaps at Chris, who's plainly desperate to hear the news, to switch the radio off. She also interrupts my weak **attempt** at small talk – *Limoges? Isn't that famous for porcelain?* "Listen, we'll have to hope that I'm not on some missing list, OK?"

"Right," I say slowly. Chris rolls his eyes and mutters something under his breath. *Now she tells us,* I think. I hadn't thought about that. If Olga's parents have officially reported her missing it's just possible that her passport number might come up when she checks in. Oh brother. I can't wait to say *au revoir* to all this.

Finally – we're at Stansted! Chris parks the car, nearly crying when he sees what it will cost us for just an hour there. Then we go with Olga into the departures hall, standing at either side of her like bodyguards, and line up at the desk for her flight. It's a very long queue. Olga plainly doesn't have much experience with queues. She sighs and looks **longingly** at the business class lounge. At least there's no sign of Uncle Dimitri.

Olga only takes off her baseball cap and sunglasses a few seconds before it's her turn to finally present her passport. She manages to smile the biggest megawatt smile she has at the lady behind the desk. Chris and me hang back, trying to look casual.

+++ attempt – Versuch +++
longing – sehnsüchtig +++

The smile seems to work. The lady does look closely at Olga's passport picture – Olga is platinum blonde in it – and asks about her hair. "Oh, I just thought blonde was *so* last year, wouldn't you agree? Your hair is *gorgeous* by the way." The woman at the desk, who has brown hair a similar colour to Olga's, is instantly charmed and Olga is *officially checked in*.

Chris and me offer to wait with Olga in the departures lounge but she just wants to go straight through to the gate. "Safer there," she says. She hasn't looked at me in a while. I actually think for a moment that she's just going to go through her departure gate without even making eye contact with us.

But finally she turns and stares at us. Her eyes are filled with tears. They might even be real ones. "I don't actually know how to thank you guys. You saved my life. Probably."

Oh, brilliant, I think I'm going to cry now, too. Chris, however, plainly doesn't want any girly tears or emotion and says firmly, "Well, you'd better go, Olga. Say hello to my mum and dad. I'll be talking to them soon." Olga nods and kisses me on both **cheeks**. She then hugs Chris and walks through the gate.

I stare after Olga for quite a long time after she's gone through. I feel strangely responsible for her. I can't explain it. This must be what *mothers* feel like, watching their children head off into the big bad world. I hear Chris say, "You'll see her again, you know that. And she'll be fine."

+++ cheek – Wange +++

I nod. Then Chris grabs me by the arm. "Oh, come on, I can't **afford** to pay for another hour in that car park!" And we run out.

+++ to afford s.th. – sich etw. leisten +++

The Breakdown

The car takes even longer to start this time. When it does start, it doesn't exactly roar like a tiger. It doesn't even roar like a ***kitten***. So by the time we're actually out of the car park almost another hour has passed. Chris doesn't quite cry as he pays for our parking but it's clear he thinks about it. He showed more emotion about the cost of that than he did about Olga leaving.

Once we're "on the road", rabbit hopping along, Chris makes a face. "You know, I didn't want to say this in front of Olga but I wasn't sure this car was going to make it here. It's on its last legs. I'm not a mechanic but I just hope we can get it back home."

Brilliant. How to explain that one to Nora – *emm, your car died on us in the middle of London!* And it's now 8.30 pm and I don't need to tell you how badly I *don't* want to be late for curfew! It's all happening again.

I lean forward in my seat, as if that might help the car to move towards our final destination. Chris is hanging over the steering wheel, too. "Only another 230,456 metres to go," says Chris. "Come on, stinky car! You can do it, baby!"

+++ kitten – Kätzchen +++

I can't help but laugh. "Wheels on Fire!" **yells** Chris.

We're now travelling at, ooh, about 12 km an hour. Cars behind us are **beeping** like crazy and Chris says, "I have to get off the road." The Citroën splutters and coughs and finally Chris stops laughing. "Oh God, it really has **clapped out** on us!" He hastily pulls over into a **layby** and the Citroën officially dies.

"Rest in Peace," says Chris slowly. "A minute's silence, please."

We can't actually *know* that the Citroën will never ride again but I think it's clear. Even if the problem does turn

+++ to yell – schreien +++ to beep – hupen +++
to clap out – den Geist aufgeben +++ layby – Parkbucht +++

out to be the battery, as Chris says vaguely it might be, I really do believe it's the end of the line.

I'm sort of glad I was with the Citroën when it happened. It's been such an important part of my life in London. Chris and me sit there in the darkness, neither of us quite knowing what to do. And as we sit there, I see a funny series of **flashbacks** in my head: Nora picking me up from the airport in this car when I arrived in London from Berlin. Nora and the Queen Mother fighting about the car when we went to get my school uniform, with the Queen Mother refusing to get inside it. Me crying on Nora's shoulder about Ed Stanton here. Nora **vanishing** in it after Grandma's funeral.

To break the silence, I tell Chris all about my memories of the Citroën and he laughs. "She is a beauty," he grins. He strokes the **dashboard** gently. "She had a good life."

"It really is sort of like another death in the family," I say quietly. Chris nods: he knows about my grandma dying. He now has his phone at his ear and is trying to reach the breakdown company listed on Nora's windscreen. He waits for someone to answer and murmurs to me: "This could be hellishly expensive."

"I have money," I mutter quickly. Then I blush. It sounds weird. I've never really been able to say that before and now it's a funny feeling. But it is nice. If this does end up costing us a **fortune**, I can probably pay for it.

+++ flashback – Rückblende +++ to vanish – verschwinden
+++ dashboard – Armaturenbrett +++
fortune – Vermögen +++

Chris doesn't respond to me as someone at the breakdown company obviously answers and he has to talk to them for a moment. They'll be here in 20 minutes or so, apparently.

20 minutes. What on earth are we going to do here in the dark for 20 minutes? And no, don't even *suggest* it. We can't even listen to the radio. We can watch planes, I suppose. You can see them taking off from here. That's what Chris seems to be doing now. "One of them must be Olga's flight," he says absently. Then he hesitates. "I need to tell you something."

And before I can react he says, "Antonia's gone back home. She's changed her mind about studying here."

I'm shocked. And, terrible though it is, I can't help but want to **punch** the air and shout YES!

Chris seems to be waiting for me to say something but I don't want to say YES! so I keep *stumm* and he goes on. "She hates London. It's just not her. Plus it's so expensive. She's made up her mind to go back to Newcastle and, well, we've agreed to take a break. You know, give each other a bit of space. She can see other people and I'm also free."

He turns and looks at me. It's a **tender** look. Forget about any breakdown company: you could probably **jump start** the Citroën's engine with the power of my emotions right now.

"You're still a bit young for me," he says slowly, with a weird smile.

+++ to punch – (mit der Faust) schlagen +++
tender – zart, weich +++ to jump start – Starthilfe geben +++

"No, you're actually wrong," I say even more slowly. "I'm *exactly* the right age and you're too old for *me*."

Chris shrugs. "I mean, it's up to you. If you think you could **handle** the **embarrassment**."

I could now describe in great detail what happens next. How Chris stares at me and how just for a second I think he's getting cold feet. Then we start kissing again and it's like I wish we could just be stuck here in Nora's dead car for all **eternity**, with the lights of airplanes rising and falling. I could tell you how embarrassed we are when a breakdown man taps on the window while *we're still kissing* and laughs at us. But that's personal, of course.

The breakdown van **tows** the Citroën back to Nora's and drops me at school at 9.57. Then there's another quick kiss, a date to meet Chris at White Out the next day is made and my life is totally and **utterly** perfect.

+++ to handle – umgehen mit +++
embarrassment – Peinlichkeit +++
eternity – Ewigkeit +++
to tow – *hier:* abschleppen +++
utterly – total +++

Von Joanna Thompson in der Reihe “Freche Mädchen – Easy English!” ebenfalls erschienen:

Girls' School – *England Calling*
Girls' School – *The Ed Affair*
Girls' School – *Season of Love*
Girls' School – *Stand by your Sam*
Girls' School – *Long Distance Kisses*
Girls' School – *Vote for Love*

Thompson, Joanna:
Girls' School – Runaway Hearts
ISBN 978 3 522 50210 8

Reihengestaltung und Gesamtausstattung: Birgit Schössow
Innentypografie: Kadja Gericke
Schrift: Minion und LTT Tapeside
Satz: KCS GmbH, Buchholz/Hamburg
Reproduktion: Medienfabrik, Stuttgart
Druck und Bindung: Friedrich Pustet, Regensburg

5 4 3 2 1°   10 11 12 13

www.planet-girl-verlag.de
www.frechemaedchen.de

Joanna Thompson
Long Distance Kisses